A GRAMMAR OF THE PERSIAN LANGUAGE

A GRAMMAR OF THE PERSIAN LANGUAGE

TO WHICH IS ADDED,

A SELECTION OF EASY EXTRACTS FOR READING,

TOGETHER WITH

A COPIOUS VOCABULARY.

By

DUNCAN FORBES, A.M.

MEMBER OF THE ROYAL ASIATIC SOCIETY OF GREAT BRITAIN AND IRELAND, MEMBER OF THE ASIATIC SOCIETY OF PARIS, AND PROFESSOR OF ORIENTAL LANGUAGES AND LITERATURE IN KING'S COLLEGE, LONDON.

SECOND EDITION,

GREATLY IMPROVED AND CONSIDERABLY ENLARGED.

GYAN

Published by

Gyan Publishing House
5, Ansari Road
Daryaganj, New Delhi-110002
Phone: 011-47034999, 9811692060
E-mail: books@gyanbooks.com

Distribution Network
gyanbooks.com
India, USA, Canada, UK, Australia, France

ISBN : 978-81-212-6212-5 (PB)
First Published, 1844

2nd Impression 2022

Printed at: Gyan Press, Delhi.

A GRAMMAR OF THE PERSIAN LANGUAGE
Author: DUNCAN FORBES

A

GRAMMAR

OF THE

PERSIAN LANGUAGE.

TO WHICH IS ADDED,

A SELECTION OF EASY EXTRACTS FOR READING,

TOGETHER WITH

A COPIOUS VOCABULARY.

BY DUNCAN FORBES, A.M.

MEMBER OF THE ROYAL ASIATIC SOCIETY OF GREAT BRITAIN AND IRELAND,
MEMBER OF THE ASIATIC SOCIETY OF PARIS,
AND PROFESSOR OF ORIENTAL LANGUAGES AND LITERATURE IN
KING'S COLLEGE, LONDON.

من طریقِ سعْي مِي آرم بجا — لَيْسَ لِلْإِنسانِ اِلّا ما سعي
دامنِ مقْصود اگر آرم بکف — از غم و أندوه مانم برطرف
ور نشُد از جهْدِ من کاري تمام — من دران معْذور باشم و آلسّلام

۱۳

SECOND EDITION,

GREATLY IMPROVED AND CONSIDERABLY ENLARGED.

1844.

TABLE OF CONTENTS.

SECTION I.

SECTION II.

SECTION III.

SECTION IV.

N.B. The Author regrets to find that the following errors, notwithstanding his care in correcting the proof-sheets, have escaped his notice till too late: — In p. 37, l. 11, *for* راسیدن, *read* رسیدن; p. 80, l. 26, *for* ختر, *read* خطر. In the Selections, Story 4, l. 2, *for* فراونست, *read* فراوانست; Story 70, l. 8, *for* پدم, *read* پدرم; the last word of the same Story should be سرای, instead of سوای.

PREFACE.

The object of the following Work is to facilitate the acquisition of a language universally allowed to be the richest and most elegant of those spoken in Modern Asia. To the general scholar, the Persian recommends itself, from its vast stores of graceful and solid literature. To the traveller in the East, a knowledge of it is as essential as that of the French used to be in Europe. Lastly, to those gallant bands of British Youth, who annually resort to India, destined to become, in their turn, the guardians of our Eastern Empire, an acquaintance with Persian is of the utmost importance. In the first place, it is the Court language of the Musulmān Princes, and that of the higher classes generally; and in the second place, a knowledge of it is requisite for the proper attainment of the Hindūstānī, or popular language, which is spoken and understood, more or less, in every part of the country.

I have been long convinced, from experience, that a work like the present is a desideratum. A Grammar of any language, adapted for a beginner, ought to be brief and perspicuous, containing only the general and more useful principles of such language. It ought to be accompanied with easy extracts for practice, as well as a copious Vocabulary. At the same time, the shortest Grammar is too long for a beginner: therefore, those parts absolutely necessary for the first reading ought to be rendered more prominent, by the use of a larger type. Lastly, the work ought to be confined entirely to its legitimate purpose—the instructing of beginners; not deviating into ingenious metaphysical and etymological discussions, however interesting in their proper place: nor should it be over-crowded with superfluous paradigms of Verbs, &c., so as to swell up the volume to an undue extent.

If this criterion of a *good* elementary Grammar is sound, which I think few men of sense will dispute, then there is ample room for the present little work, however imperfect in execution, as the first attempt of the kind that has yet been made in this country, with regard to the Persian language.

Let it not be supposed, that because this book is small in bulk it must necessarily be superficial and imperfect: نه هرچه بقامت مِهْتر بِقیمت بِهْتر. On the contrary, I am convinced that the student will here find all the information of any consequence contained in larger volumes, and a great deal which they do not contain. I have endeavoured throughout the work to enlarge upon those parts of the subject which I have observed to be most needed by beginners. Such parts of the Grammar of the Persian language as agree with our own, or with that of European languages in general, I have passed over with the utmost brevity.

The only work on the subject to which I am under any obligation is the Persian Grammar of Dr. Lumsden, Calcutta, 1810, in two folio volumes. From this valuable work I have extracted many a pearl, though it must be confessed, I was obliged often to dive through an enormous mass of water to procure it. Still, with all its metaphysics and verbosity, Dr. Lumsden's Grammar ought to be perused by every one who wishes to acquire a thorough knowledge of the Persian language. It is indeed a pity that the Work should not be reprinted in this country: it would form two octavo volumes; and, when printed in our elegant types, and on good paper, it would not look nearly so formidable and repulsive as it does in its present state.

The Selections for Reading, appended to the Grammar, consist of one hundred anecdotes, commencing with the shortest and easiest. The first seventy of them have the short vowels and the symbol *jazm* marked in full; and in the remainder the marks have been omitted, except in the case of an *izāfat*, or when there might arise an ambiguity from the omission. I have, throughout the Selections, given a species of punctuation, which the reader will find very serviceable. The *dash* (—), denotes a half-stop, like our comma, or semicolon: the *star* (*), a full stop; and the note of interrogation is the same as our own, though it might be improved by turning it backwards. Of the propriety of employing some sort of punctuation in oriental compositions there can be no doubt: the beginners will find difficulties enough to encounter, even when they know where the sentence begins and ends, which is really no unreasonable indulgence.

The greater number of the anecdotes are from Gladwin's Persian Munshī, printed in quarto about 1800, a work now very scarce. I am aware that Gladwin's anecdotes have been since reprinted, both here and on the Continent, but not in such a way as to be of any service to a beginner; for, by the use of them, he will contract a vicious mode of pronunciation, which he will afterwards have to unlearn. About thirty anecdotes, more or less, which are not in Gladwin, have been extracted from a substantial and well-written MS., a sort of Persian Joe Miller in its way, called the *Khulāsat un-nasāih*, or "the Essence of Counsels." It was my intention to have added some twenty or thirty pages of extracts from the best Persian Poets; but, on consideration, I have deferred this for the present. Should the work be deemed worthy of another edition, it is my intention to add—1st. A section on Arabic words, such as occur most frequently in Persian, confining myself merely to their mechanism, and the changes which they undergo; 2dly, A treatise on the Prosody of the language, which is greatly wanted; for without a knowledge of the various metres, much of the beauty of the Persian Poets is lost, and besides, the metre frequently assists us in detecting errors of the copyists. At the same time, the Selections and Vocabulary will be proportionally extended, by the addition of some specimens from the best Prose Writers, and extracts from the Poets.

In conclusion, let me address myself to the student as to the plan for perusing this work. In the first place, make yourself perfectly acquainted with the letters, and their various sounds; after which, endeavour to read and remember the declension of the substantives *mard* and *kitab*, pages 29 and 30; and the verb *rasīdan*, page 35. This done, read over carefully the fable, page 71, an analysis of which precedes; and, afterwards, read the two stories, pages 20 and 21, ascertaining the meaning of every word from the Vocabulary. The next step is, to read carefully all the paragraphs in the Grammar printed in large type; after which, read and translate, by the aid of the Vocabulary, the first ten or twelve pages of the Selections. Being now able to read fluently, peruse the Grammar from beginning to end. I do not mean that you should commit it to memory; but read it with such attention, that you may afterwards be able to know where to look for any rule or explanation of which you may feel the want. Lastly, preserve by you an accurate translation of every story as you proceed in the Selections; and at the end of six weeks or two months, endeavour to restore your translation back into Persian. Proceed thus till you have finished the book, and you will then find yourself possessed of a very fair elementary knowledge of the language.

D. FORBES.

8 ALFRED STREET, BEDFORD SQUARE,
August 1844.

PERSIAN GRAMMAR.

SECTION I.

ON THE LETTERS AND SYMBOLS USED IN WRITING.

1. THE Persians* have for many centuries adopted the Alphabet of the Arabs, consisting of *Twenty-eight* letters: to which they have added *four* other characters, to express sounds peculiar to their own language. These letters, then, *Thirty-two* in number, are written and read from right to left; and, consequently, their books and manuscripts begin at what we should call the *end*. Several of the letters assume different forms, according to their position in the formation of a word or a combined group; as may be seen in the following Table, Column V. Thus, in a combination of three or more letters, the first of the group, on the right-hand side, will have the form marked *Initial;* the letter or letters between the first and last will have the form marked *Medial;* and the last, on the left, will have the *Final* form. Observe, also, that in this Table, Column I. contains the names of the letters in the Persian character; II. the same in Roman character; III. the detached form of the letters, which should be learned first; and IV. the corresponding English letters.

* The Alphabet here described is used, generally speaking, by all those nations who have adopted the religion of Muhammad; viz. along the North and East of Africa, in Turkey, Arabia and Persia, and by the Mussulman portion of the people of India and Malacca.

THE PERSI-ARABIC ALPHABET.

I. NAME.	II.	III. DETACHED FORM.	IV. POWER.	V. COMBINED FORM. Final.	Med.	Initial.	VI. EXEMPLIFICATIONS. Final.		Medial.	Initial.
الِف	*alif*	ا	*a, &c.*	ا	ا	ا	وا	تا	بار	اب
بي	*be*	ب	*b*	ب	ـبـ	بـ	باب	شب	صبر	بر
پي	*pe*	پ	*p*	پ	ـپـ	پـ	آپ	چُپ	سِپر	پُر
تي	*te*	ت	*t*	ت	ـتـ	تـ	پُوت	دسْت	ستر	تپ
ثي	*se*	ث	*s*	ث	ـثـ	ثـ	رُوث	خبث	بثر	ثُور
جِيم	*jīm*	ج	*j*	ج	ـجـ	جـ	کاج	کج	شجر	جبر
چي	*che*	چ	*ch*	چ	ـچـ	چـ	کُوچ	هيچ	بچه	چُپ
حي	*'he*	ح	*h*	ح	ـحـ	حـ	رُوح	صُبْح	بحر	حر
خي	*khe*	خ	*kh*	خ	ـخـ	خـ	شاخ	يخ	تخْم	خر
دال	*dāl*	د	*d*	ـد	ـد	د	صاد	صد	فِدا	دُرّ
ذال	*zāl*	ذ	*z*	ـذ	ـذ	ذ	باذ	کاغذ	نذر	ذِمّ
ري	*re*	ر	*r*	ـر	ـر	ر	مار	مر	مرْد	رم
زي	*ze*	ز	*z*	ـز	ـز	ز	باز	گز	بزم	زر
ژي	*zhe*	ژ	*zh*	ـژ	ـژ	ژ	کاژ	پاپُژ	غژب	ژرْف
سِين	*sīn*	س	*s*	ـس	ـسـ	سـ	باس	بس	فسق	سر
شِين	*shīn*	ش	*sh*	ـش	ـشـ	شـ	پاش	پِش	نشُد	شُد
صاد	*ṣād*	ص	*s*	ـص	ـصـ	صـ	ناص	نِص	قصْد	صد

I. NAME.	II.	III. DETACHED FORM.	IV. POWER.	V. COMBINED FORM. Final.	Med.	Initial	VI. EXEMPLIFICATIONS. Final.		Medial.	Initial.
ضاد	*zâd*	ض	*z*	ـض	ـضـ	ضـ	بُعُوض	بعض	خِضر	ضِدّ
طوي	*toe*	ط	*t*	ـط	ـطـ	طـ	خُطُوط	خطّ	بطن	طي
ظوي	*zoe*	ظ	*z*	ـظ	ـظـ	ظـ	حِفاظ	حِفظ	نظر	ظفر
عَين	*aïn*	ع	*a, &c.*	ـع	ـعـ	عـ	صناع	صنع	بُعد	عسل
غَين	*ghaïn*	غ	*gh*	ـغ	ـغـ	غـ	باغ	تيغ	بِغي	غُسل
في	*fe*	ف	*f*	ـف	ـفـ	فـ	كاف	كف	سفر	فِي
قاف	*kāf*	ق	*k*	ـق	ـقـ	قـ	باق	بق	سقر	قد
كاف	*kāf*	ک	*k*	ـک	ـکـ	کـ	خاک	يک	بِکُن	کُن
گاف	*gāf*	گ	*g*	ـگ	ـگـ	گـ	راگ	رنگ	جِگر	گز
لام	*lām*	ل	*l*	ـل	ـلـ	لـ	سال	گُل	عِلم	لب
مِيم	*mīm*	م	*m*	ـم	ـمـ	مـ	تمام	سِتم	چمن	من
نُون	*nūn*	ن	*n*	ـن	ـنـ	نـ	نون	صحن	چند	نم
واو	*wāw*	و	*w, &c.*	ـو	ـو	و	رو	بو	پور	وجد
هي	*he*	ه	*h*	ـه	ـهـ	هـ	ماه	نه	بها	هُنر
يي	*ye*	ي	*y, &c.*	ـي	ـيـ	يـ	جائي	بي	حِيد	يد

Note.—The learner will observe, that the letters ا, د, ذ, ر, ز, ژ, and و do not alter in shape, whether Initial, Medial, or Final. Another peculiarity which they have, is, that they never unite with the letter following, to the left. The letters ط and ظ, in like manner, do not alter, but they always unite with the letter following on the left hand.

2. Perhaps the best mode of learning the Alphabet, is, First, to write out several times the detached or full forms of the letters in Column III. Secondly, to observe what changes (if any) these undergo, when combined in the formation of words, as exhibited in Column V. Lastly, to endeavour to transfer, into their corresponding English letters, the words given as exemplifications in Column VI.

3. In the foregoing Table, most of the letters are sufficiently represented by the corresponding English letters; (the sound of the characters چ *ch* and ش *sh* being the same as in the word *Cheshire*,) it will be necessary therefore merely to notice those that slightly differ from our own pronunciation, which are the following:

ت The sound of this letter is softer and more dental than that of the English *t:* it corresponds with the *t* of the Gaelic dialects, or that of the Italians in the word *sotto*. It corresponds with the Sanskrit त.

ث is sounded by the Arabs like our *th* hard, in the words *thick, thin;* but by the Persians and Indians it is pronounced like our *s* in the words *sick, sin*.

ح is a very strong aspirate, somewhat like our *h* in the word *haul*, but uttered by compressing the lower muscles of the throat.

خ has a sound like the *ch* in the word *loch*, as pronounced by the Scotch and Irish; or the final German *ch*, in the words *schach* and *buch*.

د is more dental than the English *d*: the former is the Sanscrit द, the latter is nearer the ड. The *d* of the Celtic dialects, and of the Italian and Spanish, corresponds with the Persian د.

ذ is properly sounded like our *th* soft, in the words *thy* and *thine;* but in Persia and India it is generally pronounced like our *z* in *zeal.*

ژ is pronounced like the *j* of the French, in the word *jour*, or our *z* in the word *azure.*

ص has a stronger or more hissing sound than our *s*. In Persia and India, however, there is little or no distinction between it and س.

ض is pronounced by the Arabs like a hard *d* or *dh;* but in Persia and India it is sounded like *z*.

ط and ظ. These letters are sounded, in Persian, like ت and ز, or very nearly so. The anomalous letter ع will be noticed hereafter.

غ has a sound somewhat like *g* in the German word *sagen*. About the banks of the Tweed, the natives sound what they fancy to be the letter *r*, very like the Eastern غ.

ق bears some resemblance to our *c* hard, in the words *calm, cup;* with this difference, that the ق is uttered from the lower muscles of the throat.

گ is sounded like our *g* hard, in *give, go;* never like our *g* in *gem, gentle.*

ن at the beginning of a word or syllable is sounded like our *n* in the word *now:* at the end of a word, when preceded by a long vowel, it sometimes has a *nasal* sound, like the French *n*, in such words as *mon* and *son*, where the effect of the *n* is to render the vowel nasal, while its own sound is scarcely perceptible.

ه is an aspirate, like our *h* in ***hand, heart;*** but at the end of a word, if preceded by the short vowel *a* (Fatha, §. 4.), the ه has no sensible sound, as in دانه *dana*, "a grain"; in which case it is called هاي مُختَفي *hāe-mukhtafī*, i.e. the *h, obscure* or *imperceptible.*

a. At the end of words derived from Arabic roots, this letter is frequently marked with two dots, thus, ة; and sounded like the letter ت *t*. In such words, when introduced into their language, the Persians generally convert the ة into ت; but sometimes they leave the ة unaltered; and frequently they omit the two dots, in which case the letter is sounded according to the general rule.

3. Much more might have been said in describing the sounds of several of the letters; but we question much whether the learner would be greatly benefited by a more detailed description. It is difficult, if not impossible, to give, in writing, a correct idea of the mere sound of a letter, unless we have one that corresponds with it in our own language. When this is not the case, we can only have recourse to such languages as happen to possess the requisite sound. It is possible, however, that the student *may be* as ignorant of these languages as of Persian. It clearly follows, then, as a general rule, that the correct sounds, of such letters as differ from our own, must be learned *by the ear*—we may say, by a *good ear;* and, consequently, a long description is needless. This remark applies in particular to the letters ت ح خ د ص ض غ ق, and the nasal ن.

OF THE PRIMITIVE VOWELS.

4. The Primitive Vowels in Arabic and Persian are three, which are expressed by the following simple notation. The first is called فَتحه *fatha,* and is written thus, َ over the consonant to which it belongs. Its sound is that of a short *a,* such as we have in the word *calamus,* which is of Eastern origin, and of which the first two syllables or root, *calam* or *kalam,* are thus written, قَلَم. Dr. Gilchrist, and several eminent Oriental scholars, have considered the *fatha* as equivalent to our short *u* in the words *sun, shun.* We have no hesitation, however, in saying, from our own experience, that our short *u* is not generally a true representation of *fatha.* In pronouncing the short *u* of *sun,* the mouth *is more shut* than in pronouncing the *a* in the words *calamus* and *calendar;* and it so happens, that the very signification of the term *fatha* is, '*open.*' In such Oriental words as we may have occasion to write in Roman characters, the *a,* unmarked, is understood always to represent the vowel *fatha,* and to have no other sound than that of *a* in *calamus* or *calendar.*

5. The second is called *kasra* كَسرہ, and is thus ِ written under the consonant to which it belongs. Its sound is generally that of our short *i* in the words *sip* and *fin,* which in Persian would be written سِپ and فِن. Occasionally it has a sound like our short *e* in the words *bed* and *fed,* which words would be most nearly represented in Persian as بِد and فِد. In India, the *kasra* has always the sound of our short *i:* the unmarked *i,* therefore,

in the course of this work, is understood to have the sound of *i* in *sip* and *fin*, in all Oriental words written in the Roman character.

6. The third is called *zamma* or *dhamma* (ضَمّه), which is thus ـُ written over its consonant. Its sound is like that of our short *u* in the words *pull* and *push*, which in Persian would be written پُل and پُش: we have its sound also in the words *foot* and *hood*, which would be written فُت and هُد. Sometimes the *zamma* has a sound approaching our short *o* in the word *solemn;* and the word گُفت *goft*, instead of *guft*, is sometimes heard with this sound. We shall, however, represent the *zamma* by the unmarked *u*, which, in all Oriental words in the Roman character, is understood to have the sound of *u* in *pull* and *push;* but never that of our *u* in such words as *use* and *perfume*, or such as *sun* and *fun*. In Persian, the three short vowels are also called *zabar*, *zer*, *pesh*, respectively.

OF THE CONSONANTS ا, ع, و, AND ي.

7. At the beginning of a word or syllable, the letter ا, like any other consonant, depends for its sound on the accompanying vowel: of itself, it is a very weak aspirate, like our *h* in the words *herb*, *honour*, and *hour*. It is still more closely identified with the *spiritus lenis* of the Greek, in such words as ἀπὸ, ἐπὶ, ὀρθός. In fact, when we utter the syllables *ab*, *ib*, and *ub*, there is a slight movement of the muscles of the throat at the commencement of utterance; and that movement the Oriental grammarians

consider to be the مَخْرَج *makhraj*, or utterance of the *consonant* ا, as in اَ *ă*, اِ *ĭ*, and اُ *ŭ*, just the same as the lips form the *makhraj* of *b*, in the syllables بَ *bă*, بِ *bĭ*, and بُ *bŭ*. Finally, the ا may be considered as the *spiritus lenis*, or weak aspirate of the letter ه.

8. The consonant ع has the same relation to the strong aspirate ح that ا has to ه; that is, the ع, like the ا, is a *spiritus lenis* or weak aspirate; but the *makhraj*, or place of utterance of ع, is in the lower muscles of the throat. With this distinction, its sound, as in the case of the letter ا, depends on the accompanying vowel, as عَب *'ab*, عِب *'ib*, عُب *'ub*, which, in the mouth of an Arab, are very different sounds from آب *ab*, إِب *ib*, and أُب *ub*. At the same time, it is impossible to explain in writing the true sound of this letter; as it is not to be found in any Euro-ropean language, so far as we know. The student who has not the advantage of a competent teacher may treat the ع as he does the ا until he has the opportunity of learning its true sound by the ear.

9. Of the consonants و and ي very little description is necessary. The letter و has generally the sound of our *w* in *we*, *went*. The modern Persians, particularly those bordering on the Turks, pronounce the و like our *v*, as in the words شَوَم *shavam* or, more nearly, *shĕvĕm*, and شوِي *shavī*, which in Eastern Persia and India are pronounced *shawam* and *shawī*. The sound of the consonant ي is exactly our own *y* in *you*, *yet*, or the German *j* in *jener*.

10. It appears, then, that the thirty-two letters constituting the Persian Alphabet are all to be considered as *consonants*, each of which may be uttered with any of the three primitive vowels, as بَ *ba*, بِ *bi*, and بُ *bu:* hence the elementary sounds of the language consist of ninety-six syllables, each consonant forming three distinct syllables.

When a consonant is accompanied by one of the three primitive vowels, it is said to be مُتَحَرِّك *mutaharrik*, that is, *moving*, or *moveable*, by that vowel. Oriental grammarians consider a syllable as a *step* or *move* in the formation of a word or sentence. In Persian and Arabic, the first letter of a word is always accompanied, or moveable, by a vowel. With regard to the following letters there is no certain rule. When, in the middle or end of a word, a consonant is not accompanied by a vowel, it is said to be ساكِن *sākin, resting* or *inert*. Thus, in the word مَرْدُمْ *mardum* the *mīm* is *moveable* by *fatha;* the *re* is *inert**, having no vowel; the *dāl* is moveable by *zamma;* and, finally, the *mīm* is *inert*. The mark ـْ or ـٛ, called جَزْم *jazm*, is placed over a consonant, to shew when it is *inert*, as in the word *mardum*, where the ر (*r*) and final م (*m*) are *inert*. As a general rule, the last letter of a Persian word is always *inert;* hence it is not necessary to mark

---

* I ought to apologize for the employing of this novel term here. In most Persian and Arabic Grammars, a letter not followed by a vowel is called *quiescent:* now, I object to the latter term, as it is apt to mislead the beginner, it being already applied in English Grammar in the sense of *not sounded*. For instance, the letter *g* is *quiescent* in the word *phlegm;* we cannot, however, say that *m* is *quiescent* in the same word, though we may say that it is *inert*. The student will be pleased to bear in mind, then, that a letter is said to be *inert* when it is not followed by a vowel.

the last letter of a word with the *jazm*. When a letter is doubled, the mark ـّـ, called *tashdīd*, is placed over it. Thus, in the word شِدَّت *shid-dat*, where the first syllable ends with د (*d*) and the next begins with د (*d*), instead of the usual mode شِدْدَت, the two *dāls* are united, and the mark ّ indicates this union.

OF THE LETTERS OF PROLONGATION, ا, و, AND ي.

11. The letters ا, و, and ي, when *inert*, serve to prolong the preceding vowel, as follows. When ا *inert* is preceded by a letter moveable by *fatha*, the *fatha* and *alif* together form a long sound like our *a* in *war*, or *au* in *haul*, which in Persian might be written وَاْر and حَاْل. Now it so happens, that the ا *inert* is always preceded by *fatha:* hence, as a general and practical rule, *alif* not beginning a word or syllable forms a sound like our *a* in *war*, or *au* in *haul*. On a similar principle, we may consider the unaspirated *h* as a letter of prolongation in the German words *wahr* and *zahl*. We may also consider the second *a* as *inert* in the words *aachen* and *waal*.

12. When the letter و *inert* is preceded by a consonant moveable by the vowel *zamma*, the *zamma* and و together form a sound like our *oo* in *tool;* which in Persian might be written طُوْل, or, which is the same thing, like our *u* in *rule*, which the Persians would write رُوْل. The same combination forms also another sound, like our *o* in *mole*, which they would write مُوْل, or, perhaps still nearer, like our *oa* in *coat*, which they would write كُوْت. In the Arabic language, the latter sound of و, viz. that of *o* in

mole, is unknown; hence grammarians call it *Majhūl*, or *'Ajamī*, *i.e.* the Unknown or Persian و; whereas the former sound, that of *u* in *rule*, is called *Ma'rūf*, the Known or Familiar و. If the letter و be preceded by a consonant moveable by *fatha*, the *fatha* and و united will form a diphthong, nearly like our *ou* in *sound*, or *ow* in *town*, but more exactly like the *au* in the German word *kaum*, which in Persian or Arabic might be written قَوْم. If the و be preceded by the vowel *kasra*, no union takes place, and the و preserves its natural sound as a consonant, as in the word سِوَا *siwā*. In English, the *w* is a letter of prolongation in many words, as *draw*, *crow*, &c.; it also contributes to the formation of a diphthong, as in *town*, *gown*, &c.

a. When the letter و is preceded by خ moveable by *fatha*, and followed by ا, the sound of و is scarcely perceptible; as in the word خواهم, pronounced *khāham*, not *khawāham*. This rule, however, applies only to words purely Persian; never to those borrowed from the Arabic language, which are very numerous.

b. In like manner, when و preceded by خ moveable by *fatha*, and sometimes by *zamma* or *kazra*, is followed by any of the letters پ, د, ر, ز, س, ش, ن, ه, or ي, the و occasionally loses its usual sound, as in the word خَود, pron. *khăd*, not *khaud* or *khawad;* so in خُود, pron. *khŭd*, not *khūd;* also in خِويش, pron. *khêsh*, not *khiwesh*. This rule also applies only to words purely Persian; and, as it is by no means general, the student must ascertain the pronunciation in such cases from a Dictionary of standard authority; such as Professor Johnson's edition of Richardson, 4to. London, 1829.

13. When the letter ي *inert* is preceded by a conso-

nant moveable by *kasra*, the *kasra* and the ي unite, and form a long vowel, like our *ee* in *feel*, which in Persian might be written فِيل; or, which is the same thing, like our *i* in *machine*, which in Persian would be written مَشِين. The same combination may also form a sound like our *ea* in *bear*, which would be written بِير, or like the French *ê* in the words *tête* and *fête;* or the German *e* followed by *h* in the words *sehr*, *gelehrt*. In the Arabic language, the latter sound of ي is unknown: hence, when the ي forms the sound of *ea* in *bear*, &c., it is called *Yāe Majhūl*, or *yāe 'Ajamī*, that is, the Unknown or Persian ي; whilst the former sound—that of *ee* in *feel*, or *i* in *machine*—is called *Yāe Ma'rūf*, the Known or Familiar ي. When the letter ي *inert* is preceded by a consonant, moveable by *fatha*, the *fatha* and the ي unite, and form a diphthong, like *ai* in the German word *Kaiser*, which in Arabic and Persian is written قَيْصَر. This sound is really that of our own *i* in *wise*, *size*, which we are pleased to call a vowel, but which, in reality, is a genuine diphthong. When the letter ي is preceded by *zamma*, no union takes place, and the ي retains its usual sound as a consonant, as in the word مُيَسَّر *muyassar*. In English, the letter *y* is a letter of prolongation in the words *say* and *key;* it also contributes to the formation of a diphthong in the word *buy*, which in Persian might be written بَيْ.

14. It appears, then, from what we have stated, that the Persian language has ten vocal sounds; viz. 1st, Three short or *primitive* vowels, as in the syllables بَد *băd;* بِد *bĭd;* بُد *bŭd*, pronounced *boŏd*. 2dly, Three corre-

sponding long vowels, formed by introducing the homogeneous letters of prolongation immediately after the preceding short vowels, as in بَاد *bād*, بِيد *bīd*, بُود *būd*. 3dly, Two diphthongs, as in بَيْد *baid*, the *ai* pronounced like our *i* in *abide;* and بَوْد *baud*, the *au* pronounced like our *ou* in *loud.* 4thly, The two long vowels, peculiarly Persian, or *Majhūl*, as بِيل *bêl*, pronounced like the English word *bail*, and رُوز *rôz*, pronounced very nearly like the English word *rose*.

15. It must be observed, that there are very few Persian works, manuscript or printed, in which all the vowels are marked as we have just described. The primitive short vowels are almost always omitted, as well as the marks ـْ *jazm* and ـّ *tashdid;* nor is the omission of any consequence to the natives and those who know the language. To the young beginner, however, in this country, it is essential to commence with books having the vowels carefully marked; otherwise, he will contract a vicious mode of pronunciation, which he will find it difficult afterwards to unlearn. At the same time, it is no easy matter in printing to insert all the vowel-points &c. in a proper and accurate manner. In the present work, a medium will be observed, which, without over-crowding the text with marks, will suffice to enable the learner to read without any error, provided he will attend to the following rules.

16. In the first place,—the last letter of every word (as already mentioned, §. 10.) is *inert:* hence the mark

ـْ *jazm* is in that case dispensed with: when there is an exception to this rule, as in the formation of the genitive case, the last letter will be marked with the requisite vowel. Secondly, the letters ا, و, and ي, not initial, are generally *inert;* hence, they are not in such cases marked with the *jazm:* whenever و and ي, not initial, are moveable consonants, they are marked with the requisite vowels. Thirdly, to distinguish between the *majhūl* and *ma'rūf* sounds of و and ي, the following rule is observed. When و and ي follow a consonant, unmarked by a short vowel or *jazm*, they are understood to have the *majhūl* sound, or that of ō and ê respectively, as in مور *mōr*, "an ant," and شير *shêr*, "a lion." If, on the other hand, the consonant preceding و have the vowel ـُ, and that preceding ي the vowel ـِ, they have the *ma'rūf* sound, or that of *u* in *rule* and *i* in *machine* respectively, as in the words سُود *sūd*, "gain," and شِير, *shīr*, "milk": and if the preceding consonant be marked with *jazm*, و and ي are consonants. Fourthly, the short vowel *fatha* ـَ is of more frequent occurrence than the other two: hence it is omitted in the printing; and the learner is to supply it for every consonant except the last, provided he see no other vowel, nor the mark *jazm* accompanying any of the consonants aforesaid. The vowel *fatha* is written before the letters و and ي when they form diphthongs, as in قَوم *kaum*, "a tribe," and سَير *sair* (pronounced like the English word *sire*), "a walk." According to this method, the ten vocal sounds will be uniformly represented as follows, both in the Persian text, and in such Persian words as we may have occasion to write in Roman characters. 1st, Three short vowels, بَر *bar*, بِن *bin*, سُر *sur*. 2dly, Three corresponding long, بار *bār*, بِين *bīn*, سُور *sūr*. 3dly, Two diphthongs, سَير *saīr*, قَوم *kaum*. 4thly, The two sounds called *Majhūl*, not used in Arabic, بيل *bēl*, روز *rōz*.

17. The letters ا and ع, beginning a word or syllable, form, according to our notions, an initial vowel; although the Orientals deny the possibility of such a thing: thus—

اد اِد اُد; ااد or آد اِيد اُود; اَيد اَود; ايد اود

ad id ud; ād īd ūd; aid aud; ēd ōd;

or,

عد عِد عُد; عاد عِيد عُود; عَيد عَود.

'ad 'id 'ud; 'ād 'īd 'ūd; 'aid, 'aud.

Instead of writing two *alifs* at the beginning of a word, as in ااد *ād*, it is usual (except in Dictionaries) to write one *alif* with the other curved over it; thus, آد. This symbol ~ is called مدّة *madda*, "extension," and denotes that the *alif* is sounded long, like our *a* in *water*.

a. The learner will recollect, that the sounds commencing with ع must be uttered with the lower muscles of the throat. In other respects he may view the ا and ع in any of the three following lights. 1st, He may consider them of the same value as the *spiritus lenis* (᾿) in such Greek words as ἀν, ἐν, &c. 2dly, He may consider them as equivalent to the letter *h* in the English words *hour, herb, honour*, &c. Lastly, he may consider them as mere blocks, whereupon to place the vowels requisite to the formation of the syllable. Practically speaking, then, ا and ع *when initial*, and و and ي *when not initial*, require the beginner's strictest attention, as they all contribute in such cases to the formation of several sounds.

b. It further appears, that when, in Persian, a word or syllable begins with what we consider to be a vowel, such words or syllables must have the letter ا or ع to start with. Throughout this work, when we have occasion to write such words in the Roman character, the corresponding place of the ع will be indicated by an apostrophe or *spiritus lenis;* thus, عسل *'asal,* عابد *'ābid,* بعد *ba'd,* to distinguish the same from اسل *asal,* آبد *ābid,* بد *bad,* باد *bād.*

18. When one syllable of a word ends with a vowel, and, according to our ideas of orthography, the following syllable begins with a vowel, that is, virtually, with an ا in Persian, the mark ء (sometimes ئ) *hamza* is used instead of the ا; thus, پائی *pā-e,* instead of پاای; فائده *fa-idah,* instead of فاِاده.

a. The sound of the mark *hamza,* according to the Arabian Grammarians, differs in some degree from the letter ا, being somewhat akin to the letter ع, which its shape ء would seem to warrant; but in Persian this distinction is overlooked. According to the strict rule, the *hamza* ought to be used whenever a syllable, beginning with a vowel, is added to a root, in the way of inflexion or derivation, as دیدئیم *dīdem,* "*we saw,*" from دید; بدئی *bad-ī,* "*badness,*" from بد *bad;* but this rule is seldom or never observed. Practically speaking, then, in Persian the *hamza* in the middle of a word is nearly of the same import as our hyphen (with which it may be represented in the Roman characters), in such words as *re-open,* which in the Persian character might be written رئوپن. At the end of words terminating with the imperceptible *h* ه, or ی, the *hamza* has the sound of *e* or *i,* long or short, as will be observed hereafter.

†19. As words and phrases from the Arabic language enter very freely into Persian composition, we cannot well

omit the following remarks. Arabic nouns have frequently the definite article ال (*the*) of that language prefixed to them; and if the noun happens to begin with any of the thirteen letters, ت, ث, د, ذ, ر, ز, س, ش, ص, ض, ط, ظ, or ن, the ل of the article assumes the sound of the initial letter of the noun, which is then marked with *tashdīd;* thus, اَلنُّورُ *the light,* pronounced *an-nūru,* not *al-nūru.* But in these instances, although the ل has lost its own sound, it must always be written in its own form. Of course, when the noun begins with ل, the ل of the article coincides with it in like manner, as in the words اَللَّيْلَةُ *al-lailatu,* "the night"; and in this case the ل of the article is sometimes omitted, and the initial *lām* of the noun marked by *tashdīd,* as اَلَّيْلَةُ *al-lailatu.*

a. We have already noticed (page 6) the anomalous character ة, which is common in Arabic derivatives, and sounded like the letter ت, into which it is often changed in Persian. The thirteen letters, ت &c., above mentioned, together with the letter ل, are, by the Arabian Grammarians, called *solar* or *sunny* letters, because, forsooth, the word شَمْس *shams,* "the sun," happens to begin with one of them. The other letters of the Arabic alphabet are called *lunar,* because, we presume, the word قمر *kamar* "the moon" begins with one of the number, or simply because they are *not solar.* Of course, the captious critic might find a thousand equally valid reasons for calling them by any other term, such as *gold* and *silver, black* and *blue,* &c.; but we merely state the fact as we find it.

† 20. In general, the Arabic nouns of the above description, when introduced into the Persian language, are in a state of construction with another substantive which

precedes them; like our Latin terms "*jus gentium*," "*vis inertiæ*," &c. In such cases, the last letter of the first or governing word is moveable by the vowel *zamma*, which serves for the enunciation of the ا following; and, at the same time, the ا is marked with the symbol ـٙ, called وَصْلَه *wasla*, to denote such union; as in the words اميرُ ٱلمومِنين *Amīr-ul-mūminīn*, "Commander of the Faithful;" اِقبالُ ٱلدَّولَه *Ikbāl-ud-daula*, "The dignity of the state."

a. Arabic nouns occasionally occur in Persian having their final letters marked with the symbol called *tanwīn*, which signifies the using of the letter ن. The *tanwīn*, which in Arabic grammar serves to mark the inflexions of a noun, is formed by doubling the vowel-point of the last letter, which indicates at once its presence and its sound; thus, بابٌ *bābun*, بابٍ *bābin*, باباً *bāban*. The last form requires the letter ا, which does not, however, prolong the sound of the final syllable. The ا is not required when the noun ends with a *hamza* or the letter ة, as شَيْءً *shai-an*, حِكْمَةً *hikmatan*; or when the word ends in ي *ya*, surmounted by ا (in which case the ا only is pronounced), as هُدىً *hudan*. In words ending in ي, surmounted by ا, without the *tanwīn* or *nūnation*, the *alif* is sounded like the *alif* of prolongation, as تعالي *ta'ālā*, عُقْبي *'ukbā*, &c.

21. The eight letters, ث, ح, ص, ض, ط, ظ, ع, and ق, are peculiar to the Arabic language: hence, as a general rule, a word containing any one of these letters may be considered as borrowed from the Arabic: and should it include the long vowels و or ي, they cannot have the *majhūl* sound, except it be the ي (*e*) of *unity* (of which more hereafter) added at the end. The four letters پ, چ, ژ, and گ, are not used in the Arabic language: hence, a

word in which any one of them occurs may be considered as purely Persian. The remaining twenty letters are common to both languages.

The three following Stories are intended as an Exercise in Reading and Writing for the Learner. The first is given both in the Persian and Roman characters. The second is given in the Persian character alone; and the Learner is to turn the same into the corresponding English letters. The third is in the Roman character; which the Student, by a little attention to all that has preceded, ought to turn into the proper Persian character. It is essential that he should be able to read the latter fluently, before he proceeds further with this work. A Literal Translation is added to each.

Before commencing, however, the Learner had better reconsider all that has gone before, and be sure that he thoroughly recollects the meaning of the following symbols: ـَ, ـِ, ـُ, ـْ, ـّ, ـٔ, آ and أ, as well as the different sounds which ا, ع, و and ي contribute to form.

STORY I.

روزي خُسرُو پَروِيز کِه شِيرِين زَوجهٔ مَحبُوبهٔ او بُود—

گُفت—خُوش چِيزي اَست کِه پادشاهِي دايِم بُودي *

شِيرِين گُفت—اگر دايِم بُودي بتُو نرسِيدي *

THE SAME IN ROMAN CHARACTERS.

Roze Khusrū Parwīz ki Shīrīn zauja-i mahbūba-i ō būd, guft, khush chīze ast ki badshāhī dā-īm būde. Shīrīn guft, agar dā-īm būde batū narasīde.

TRANSLATION.

One day, Khusrū Parwīz, whose beloved wife was Shīrīn, said, "What a pleasant thing it were if Royalty were everlasting!"

Shīrīn said, "If it had been everlasting, it would not have come to thee."

N.B. Observe, that the final ه (vide p. 6) in the words كه, زَوجه, &c., having no perceptible sound, is omitted in the Roman character.

STORY II.—TO BE TURNED INTO THE ROMAN CHARACTER.

مردي براي ديدنِ شخصي به خانهٔ او به وقتِ
چاشتِ دو پهر آمد — آن شخص در خانهٔ خود از راهِ
غرفه ميديد كه اين مرد ميآيد — به نوكرانِ خود گفت
— همانگاه بپرسد كه صاحبِ خانه كجاست — شما
بگوئيد كه همين زمان بخانهٔ كسي مهمان رفته اند —
همان گاه او آمده پرسيد كه صاحبِ خانه كجاست گفتند
همين ساعت بيرون رفته اند — گفت عجب احمق است
كه در اين وقتِ گرما از خانهٔ خود رفته است — صاحبِ
خانه سر از دريچه برآورده گفت احمق توئي كه اين وقت
ميگردي — من در خانهٔ خود خوش نشسته ام

TRANSLATION.

A man went, for the purpose of seeing a certain person, to his house, at the time of the midday meal. That person, in his own house, saw this man coming. He said to his servants, "When he asks where the master of the house is, you will say that he is now gone to dine with some one." In the mean while, the man having arrived, asked, "Where is the master of the house?" They said,

"He is just this moment gone out." The man said, "A rare fool he is, to have gone out of his house at such a sultry hour." The master of the house, putting his head out of the window, said, "You are a fool, to wander about at this time. I am comfortably reposing in my own house."

STORY III.—TO BE TURNED INTO THE PERSIAN CHARACTER.

Dihkāne khare dāsht. Az sababi bekharjī, khar rā barā-e charīdan babāghe sar mīdād. Mardumāni bāgh khar rā mīzadand wa, az zarā'at ba dar mīkardand. Roze dihkān posti sher rā bar khar bast wa guft "wakti shab barā-e charīdan tū bar ā-ī, wa, āwāz makun." Hamchunān har shab bā posti sher ān khar babāgh mīraft. Harkĭ ba shab mīdīd, yakīn mīdānist ki īn sher ast. Shabe bāghbān orā dīd, wa az tars bar bālā-e darahkte raft. Dar asnā-e ān, khare dīgar ki dar ān nazdīkī būd āwāz kard, wa khari dihkān nīz ba āwāz dar āmad, wa bang zadan misli kharān girift. Bāghbān orā shinākht wā dānist ki īn kīst. Az darakht farod āmad, wa ān khar rā bisyar lat bazad. Az īnjā khiradmandān gufta and ki "kharān rā khāmoshī bih."

TRANSLATION.

A certain villager had an ass, which, for the sake of economy, he used to let loose in a certain garden, for the purpose of grazing. The people of the garden used to beat the beast, and drive him from the cultivated ground. One day, the villager fastened a lion's skin on the ass, and said (so goes the story): "At the time of night, you go forth to graze, and do not make a noise." Even so, every night, in the lion's skin, the ass used to go into the garden: whoever saw him by night, used to think for certain that it was a lion. One night the gardener saw him, and from fear he went up into a tree. In the mean time, another ass, which was in that neighbourhood, made a noise; and the ass of the villager also raised his voice, and began to bray, just like any other donkey. The gardener recognised him, and knew what he was. He came down from the tree, and gave the ass a sound beating with a stick.—On this subject the wise have said, "For the ass, silence is best."

In turning the preceding story into the Persian character, the student will observe, that *t*, *s*, *z*, *k* and *h*, are to be turned into ت, س, ز, ك and ه, respectively; the exceptions being the *k* of *dihkān*, which is ق, and the *s* of *misli*, which is ث. The combinations *ch*, *kh*, *sh*, and *gh*, are چ, خ, ش, and غ, respectively. He will of course attend to the *initial*, *medial*, and *final* forms of the letters, according to circumstances. Let him also remember, that every letter must be joined in the same word to the one following it on the left, except ا, د, ذ, ر, ز, ژ, and و; after any of which there is a blank, and the next letter is of the initial form.

+22. We may here mention, that the twenty-eight letters of the Arabic language are also used (chiefly in recording the dates of historical events) for the purpose of Numerical computation. The Numerical order of the Letters, however, in this case, differs from that given in the Alphabet; being, in fact, the identical arrangement of the Hebrew, so far as the latter extends, viz. to the letter ت, 400. The following is the order of the Numerical Alphabet with the corresponding number placed above each letter; the whole being grouped into eight unmeaning words, to serve as a *memoria technica*.

ضظغ	ثخذ	قرشت	سعفص	كلمن	حطي	هوز	ابجد
800 900 1000	500 600 700	100 200 300 400	60 70 80 90	20 30 40 50	8 9 10	5 6 7	1 2 3 4

where ا denotes one, ب two, ج three, د four, &c.

a. In reckoning, by the preceding system, the four letters peculiarly Persian (21), viz. پ, چ, ژ and گ, have the same value as their cognate Arabic letters of which they are modifications, that is, of ب, ج, ز, and ك, respectively. The mode of recording any event is, to form a brief sentence, such, that the numerical values of all the letters, when added together, amount to the year (of the Hijri) in which the event took place. Thus, the death of Ahlī of Shīrāz, who may be considered as the last of the Classic Poets of Persia, happened in A. H. 942. This date is recorded in the sentence بادشاه شعرا بود اهلي, *i. e.* "Ahlī was the king of poets;" which at the same time contains a high compliment to the merits of the deceased. The following date, on the death of the renowned Hyder Ali of Maisūr (A. H. 1196), is equally elegant, and much more poetic. The reader will bear in mind that *Bālāghāt*, is the scene of one of Hyder's most celebrated victories; hence the appropriateness of the following well-chosen expression:

جان بالا گهات برفت

"The spirit of Bālāghāt is gone."

b. In Arabia and Persia, the art of printing is as yet very little used: hence their books, as was once the case in Europe, are written in a variety of different hands. Of these, the most common are, 1st, the *Naskhī* نسخي, of which the type employed in the two Stories, pages 20 and 21, is a very good imitation. Most Arabic Manuscripts, and particularly those of the Korān, are in this hand; and from its compact form, it is generally used in Europe for printing books in the Arabic, Persian, Turkish, and Hindūstānī languages. 2dly, The *Ta'līk* تعليق, a beautiful hand, used chiefly by the Persians in disseminating copies of their more-esteemed authors. In India, the Ta'līk has been extensively employed for printing, both in Persian and Hindūstānī; and within the last twenty years, a few Persian works, in the same hand, have issued from the Pāshā of Egypt's press at Būlāk. 3dly, The *Shikasta* شكسته, or *broken* hand, which is used in correspondence. It is quite irregular, and unadapted for printing; but not inelegant in appearance, when properly written. For a more ample account of this subject, see "Essai de Calligraphie Orientale," in the Appendix to Herbin's "Développements des Principes de la Langue Arabe," 4to. Paris, 1803.

SECTION II.

ON SUBSTANTIVES, ADJECTIVES, AND PRONOUNS.

23. It is considered by the Grammarians of Arabia and Persia that there are only Three Parts of Speech — the Noun اسم *Ism*, the Verb فعل *Fi'l*, and the Particle حرف *Harf.* Under the term Noun, they include Substantives, Adjectives, Pronouns, Participles, and Infinitives: their Verb agrees in its nature with ours; and their Particle includes Adverbs, Prepositions, Conjunctions, and Interjections.

a. In the present work we shall of course adhere to that division of the Parts of Speech which is followed in the Latin Grammar, with which the Student is supposed to be acquainted.

OF GENDER.

24. In the Persian language, the Gender of Nouns agrees exactly with that of the same Part of Speech in English; males being masculine, females feminine, and all other words neuter.

a. Animals have either different names to express male and female; as, پسر *pisar*, "a son"; دختر *dukhtar*, "a daughter": or the terms نر *nar* (male), and ماده *māda* (female), added or prefixed, serve the same purpose; as, شیرِ نر *sher-i-nar*, "a lion," شیرِ ماده *sheri-māda*, "a lioness"; so, نرگاو *nar-gāw*, "a bull," ماده‌گاو *māda-gāw*, "a cow."

FORMATION OF THE PLURAL NUMBER.

25. In Persian there are two Numbers—the Singular and the Plural. As a general rule, Masculines and Femi-

nines form the Plural, by adding ان *ān* to the Singular; and inanimate objects, or Neuters, form the Plural, by adding ها *hā*; as, جانور *jānwar*, "animal," plur. جانوران *jānwarān*; چيز *chīz*, "a thing," plur. چيزها *chizhā*.

a. This simple and general rule is subject to some modification, which may be expressed as follows:—Names applicable to persons, and epithets descriptive of rational beings, make the plural almost invariably in ان; as, مرد *mard*, "man," pl. مردان *mardān*, "men"; زن *zan*, "a woman," pl. زنان *zanān*, "women"; دل فريب *dil-fireb*, "an allurer of hearts," pl. دل فريبان *dil-firebān*. Names of animals not rational, form the plural, generally, by adding ان—, but often by ها; as, اسپ *asp*, "a horse," pl. اسپان *aspān*; شتر *shutur*, "a camel," pl. شتران *shuturān*, or شترها *shuturhā*, "camels." Names of inanimate objects add ها generally, sometimes ان—; as, قلم *kalam*, "a pen," pl. قلمها *kalamhā*, "pens"; درخت *darakht*, "a tree," pl. درختها *darakhtā*, "trees," and sometimes درختان.

b. When nouns ending in the obscure *h* ه (page 6) have occasion to add ان—, the ه is converted into گ; as, فرشته *firishta*, "an angel," pl. فرشتگان *firishtagān*, "angels": and sometimes the ه is retained, with the گ; as, مرده "dead," pl. مردهگان. When such nouns have occasion to add ها, the final ه of the singular disappears; as, نامه *nāma*, "a book or letter," pl. نامها *nāmahā*. When nouns ending in ا (*ā*) or و (*ū* or *ō*) have occasion to add ان—, the letter ي (*y*) is inserted, to avoid a hiatus; as, دانا *dānā*, "a sage," pl. دانايان *dānāyān*; so, پري رو *pari-rū*, "fairy-faced," pl. پري رويان *parī-rūyān*, "the fairy-faced ones": and sometimes, though rarely, the letter ي is omitted after و; as, بازو "the arm," pl. بازوان *bazūān* or *bazuwān*.

c. Arabic nouns sometimes form their plurals according to rules peculiar to that language, which will be briefly noticed in the Appendix.

DECLENSION OF NOUNS.

26. Persian Nouns undergo no change corresponding to the various Cases of the Greek and Latin. The term *Case* however is here retained, as it forms the simplest means for explaining how the various relations of Substantives are expressed in this language.

The *Genitive* or *Possessive Case* is formed by the juxtaposition of two substantives; where the *regimen,* or thing possessed, comes always first, having its final letter sounded with the vowel *kasra* (*i*)—called كَسْرهٔ اِضافت *Kasra-i Izāfat,* "The *kasra* of relationship";—thus, پِسرِ مَلِك *pisar-i-malik,* "The son of the king (*filius regis*)"; so كِتابِ پِسرِ مَلِك *kitāb-i pisar-i malik,* "The book of the son of the king (*liber filii regis*)." If the governing word ends in the long vowels ا (*ā*) or و (*ū* or *ō*), instead of these letters being followed by the *kasra* (or short *i*), as above, the letter ي (*majhūl*) with the mark *hamza* (§.18.) is used; as, پائي مَرْد *pā-e mard,* "The foot of the man"; رُوئي پِسر *rū-e pisar,* "The face of the boy." If the governing word ends with the obscure ه (*h*), or the long vowel ي (*ī* or *e*), the mark *hamza,* with the vowel *kasra* (expressed or understood) is used; as, خانهٔ مَرْد *khāna-i mard,* "The house of the man"; ماهِيءِ دَرْيا *māhī-i daryā,* "The fish of the sea."

a. In English we form the Possessive Case in two ways; thus, "The king's son," or "The son of the king": the latter mode agrees exactly with that of the Persian; and the vowel *kasra* &c. (*i* &c.), added to the governing word in Persian, corresponds to the particle *of* in English. Hence, in turning English into Persian, should a complex string of words related to each other in the genitive case occur, the student has, in the first place, to resolve the same in his mind into that form of the genitive case which is made by the particle *of* in English; then convert them into Persian in the very same order, inserting the proper marks of the *izāfat*. Thus, to assume an extreme case, we shall suppose the student has to express in Persian, "The colour of the king of Irān's horse's head." Let him, in the first place, endeavour to express the plain meaning of the phrase in English, by the aid of the particle *of* alone; thus, "The colour of the head of the horse of the king of Irān": then the Persian will easily follow; as, رنگِ سرِ اسپِ بادشاهِ ایران, *rang-i sar-i asp-i bad-shāh-i Irān;* the order being the same.

b. The words صاحِب *sahib*, denoting "possessor," and سر *sar*, denoting "source," when united with another word, generally omit the *kasra*; as, صاحِب دِل *sahib-dil*, "a sage" (homme d'esprit); so سرمایه *sar māya*, "the source of wealth," or "capital in trade."

27. *Dative and Accusative*, &c.—The syllable را is added to a noun, when it stands in that relation to a verb which corresponds with the Dative or Accusative of the Latin; as, مَردرا کِتاب دادم *mardrā kitāb dādam* (viro librum dedi), "I gave the book to the man"; اسپرا دِیدم *aspra dīdam* (equum vidi), "I saw the horse": but the Dative is frequently formed by the Preposition به, instead of the affix را; and the Accusative is often the same as the Nominative, as will be more fully shewn in the Syntax.—The *Vocative*

is formed, as in English, by placing some Interjection before the Nominative; as, اي مرد *Ai mard!* "O man!" In poetry, and also in prose compositions denoting prayer or supplication, the Vocative is frequently formed by adding ا *ā* to the Nominative; as, بلبلا *bulbulā!* "O nightingale!" دوستا *dostā!* "O friend!"—The *Ablative* is formed, as in English, by prefixing the Prepositions از *az*, "from" or "by," در *dar*, "in," &c., to the Nominative; as, از مرد *az mard*, "from the man"; در خانه *dar khāna*, "in the house."—The Cases of the Plural Number are formed exactly in the same way.

28. To conform with the mode of European Grammars, we shall add two examples of the Declension of a Persian Noun.

مرد *Mard*, "Man."

	SINGULAR.	PLURAL.
Nom.	مرد ***mard; vir,*** "man," "the man."	مردان ***mardān; viri,*** "men."
Gen.	ـِ مرد* ***i-mard; viri,*** "of man," &c.	ـِ مردان ***i-mardān; virorum,*** "of men."
Dat.	مرد را ***mard-rā; viro,*** "to man."	مردان را ***mardān-ra; viris,*** "to men."
Acc.	مرد را ***mard-rā; virum,*** "man."	مردان را ***mardān-ra; viros,*** "men."
Voc.	اي مرد ***ai mard; vir,*** "O man!"	اي مردان ***ai mardān; viri,*** "O men!"
Abl.	از مرد ***az mard; viro,*** "from man."	از مردان ***az mardān; viris,*** "from men."

* The symbol ـِ before the Genitive Case merely indicates the place of the governing word, the last letter of which must have the vowel ـِ (ء or ي), as explained in Sect. 26.

كِتاب *Kitāb*, "A Book."

SINGULAR.			PLURAL.	
Nom.	كِتاب	*kitāb*, "a book," "the book."	كِتابها	*kitābhā*, "books."
Gen.	ــِـ كِتاب	*i-kitāb*, "of a book."	ــِـ كِتابها	*i-kitābhā*, "of books."
Dat.	كِتابرا	*kitāb-rā*, "to a book."	كِتابهارا	*kitābhā-rā*, "to books."
Acc.	كِتابرا	*kitāb-rā*, "the book."	كِتابهارا	*kitābhā-rā*, "books."
Voc.	اي كِتاب	*ai kitāb*, "O book!"	اي كِتابها	*ai kitābhā*, "O books!"
Abl.	از كِتاب	*az kitāb*, "from a book."	از كِتابها	*az kitābhā*, "from books."

a. In like manner may be declined every Substantive in the Persian language. The only questions are, in the first place, whether ــِـ, ي, or ء, will be used as the sign of the *izāfat* or Genitive Case; which is easily solved by the rule laid down in Sect. 26; the choice depending on the last syllable of the preceding or governing word; and, secondly, whether ان or ها is to be added in the plural, which is decided by a careful perusal of Sect. 25.

29. In Persian, there is no word corresponding exactly to our Definite Article *the;* so that common names, as مَرْد *mard*, may signify "man," or "the man," according to circumstances, which the context will generally indicate. A common substantive in the singular number, however, is restricted to unity, by adding the lettter ى (*majhūl*) to it; as, مَرْدي *mard-e*, "one man," or "a certain man."

a. The same letter, ي, added to nouns (plural as well as singular), followed by the particle كه, indicating a relative clause of a sentence, seems to have the effect of our *definite article;* thus, كساني كه بقُوّت ازمن بيش اند "The (or Those) persons who in power are my superiors."—Anwari Suhaili, Book III. So in the following passage from Sa'dī's Gulistan, Book I.: ابلهي كو روزِ روشن شمعِ كافوري نِهد "The (or That) fool who in bright day sets up (burns) a camphor candle." Sometimes the ي *majhūl* added to a noun gives it a sense of excess or universality; as in Hafiz, عِشق آفتي اسْت "Love is one (excessive) calamity": so, عالي "The whole world": خلقي "The whole nation *or* people." Words ending in the obscure ه add a *hamza,* instead of the ي (*majhūl*); as, خانهٔ *khana-e,* "one house"; where the *hamza* has the same sound as the ي which it represents.

OF ADJECTIVES.

30. Persian Adjectives are indeclinable; and in construction, they follow the substantives which they qualify; at the same time, the last letter of the substantive must have the *kasra* ـِ (or ى, or ء) superadded, as in the formation of the Genitive Case (§. 26.): thus, مَرْدِ نيك *mard-i nek,* "a good man"; عُمْرِ دراز *'umr-i darāz,* "a long life"; رُوي خُوب *rū-e khūb,* "a fair face"; بنْدهٔ وفادار *banda-e-wafādār,* "a faithful slave." The only variation which Persian Adjectives undergo is that of comparison, in which respect they very much resemble the same part of speech in English. The Comparative Degree is formed regularly, by adding to the Positive the syllable تَر *tar;* and the Superlative, by adding تَرِين *tarīn:* thus, خُوب *khūb,* "fair," خُوبْتَر *khūb-tar,* "fairer," خُوبْتَرِين *khūb-tarīn,* "fairest."

a. The terminations تر and ترِين may be joined to the Adjective, or written separately, at pleasure: thus, in the above example, we might write خُوب تر and خُوب ترِین.

b. When an Arabic adjective occurs in Persian, it is compared frequently in the preceding manner; as, فضل "excellent," فضلتر "more excellent," &c.: but sometimes the comparison is effected as in Arabic; thus, افضل "more *or* most excellent"; and occasionally we meet with both forms united, as افضلتر. When an adjective is used as a noun, it forms the plural in accordance with the substantive represented; as, نیکان "the good," خُوبان "the fair," &c.; دادها "things given," from the participle داده *dāda*.

OF PRONOUNS.

31. The Personal Pronouns are the following:

SINGULAR.

PERS.	NOMINATIVE.			ACCUSATIVE & DATIVE.		
1.	من	*man*, "I."		مرا	*marā*, "me," "to me."	
2.	تُو	*tū*, "thou."		تُرا	*tura*, "thee," "to thee."	
3.	او	*o*,	"he," "she."	اورا	*orā*,	"him," "her," *or* "to him," "to her."
	وَي	*wai*,		وَيرا	*wairā*,	
Neut.	آن	*ān*, "it," "that."		آنرا	*ānrā*, "it," *or* "to it."	

PLURAL.

1.	ما	*mā*, "we."		مارا	"us," "to us."
2.	شُما	*shumā*, "you."		شُمارا	"you," "to you."
3.	ایشان	*eshān*,	"they," *or* "those."	ایشانرا	"them," "to them."
Neut.	آنها	*ānhā*,		آنهارا	"those," "to those."

a. The inflection of the personal pronouns differs in no respect from that of nouns; the words مرا and تُرا being clearly contractions of منرا and تُورا. They all form the Genitive Case, like the substantives, by placing the governing word, with the sign of the *izāfat*, before the nominatives (sing. or plur.) of the pronouns; as, پدرِ من *padar-i man*, "my father"; اسپِ تُو *asp-i tū*, "thy horse"; کتابِ او *kitābi o*, "his *or* her book"; قیمتِ آن *kīmat-i ān*, "its price"; خانهٔ ما *khana-e mā*, "our house," &c. The second person forms the Vocative by prefixing an interjection; as, اَي تُو *ai tū*, "O thou!" The first and third persons cannot, in their nature, have a Vocative, without virtually becoming the second person. They all form the Ablative by prefixing the simple prepositions از, در, با, &c. to the Nominative; as, ازمن *az man*, "from me"; با تُو *bā tū*, "with thee"; براو *bar ō*, "on him"; درآن *dar ān*, "in it."

32. Besides the regular inflexions of the Personal Pronouns, there are certain contracted forms or affixes, which, when joined to nouns or verbs, may denote the Genitive, Dative, or Accusative Case. These are, ـَم *am*, for the 1st person; ـَت *at*, for the 2d; and ـَش *ash*, for the 3d; as, دِلم *dil-am*, "my heart"; سرت *sar-at*, "thy head"; دستش *dast-ash*, "his hand": but the explanation of these, as well as of the Reciprocal Pronoun خُود *khud*, or خويش *khesh* (§. 12. *b.*), "self," or "selves," belongs more properly to the section on Syntax.

33. The Demonstrative or Adjective Pronouns are, اين *īn*, "this" or "these," and آن *ān*, "that" or those." As Adjectives, they are indeclinable, and applicable to all

genders and numbers; thus, اِین مرْد *īn mard,* "this man"; اِین مرْدان *īn mardān,* "these men"; آن کِتاب *ān kitāb,* "that book"; آن کِتابها *ān kitābhā,* "those books." When used as the representatives of nouns, they form the plural, in the same manner as the noun for which they stand; thus, اِینان *īnān,* "these" or "they," if applicable to persons; and اِینها *inhā,* "these" or "they," when referring to inanimate things; and in like manner آنان and آنها "those" or "they."

34. The Interrogative Pronouns are کِه *ki* (Dative and Accusative, کِرا *kirā*), "who?" "whom?" and چِه *chi* (Dative and Accusative, چِرا *chirā*), "what?" "which?" They are applicable to both numbers; the former generally relating to persons, and the latter to things. To these may be added, کُدام *kudām,* "Which of two?" or "Which out of any number?" چند *chand,* "how many?" also, "some" or "several," which are equally applicable to persons and inanimate things. When کِه and چِه are added to the word هر *har* or هران *har-ān,* they correspond to our *who-, what-,* or *which-soever;* as, هرکِه *harki,* or هرآنْکِه *harānkī,* "whosoever," &c. Finally, کِه and چِه are sometimes used as substitutes for the Relative Pronouns, of which more hereafter.

a. The Persian language, like the Arabic, generally dispenses with, or rather does not possess, a relative pronoun exactly similar to the *qui, quæ, quod* of the Latin. For instance, "The man whom I saw," *Vir quem vidi,* would be expressed in Persian آن مرد که اورا دیدم *an mard ki ora dīdam*"; or, آن مرد که دیدمش *an mard ki dīdamash;* literally, "The man that I saw him." In these expressions it will be seen that the particle که is not a relative pronoun, but a conjunction. This remark, which may be considered premature, is sufficient to shew that the explanation of this peculiarity belongs more properly to the Syntax.

SECTION III.

ON THE VERB.

35. The Persian Verb is extremely regular in its structure; there being only *one form* or *conjugation,* applicable to every verb in the language. All the Tenses are formed either from the Root or from the Infinitive, as will be seen in the following example of the verb رسیدن *rasīdan,* "to arrive." The root of this verb is رس *ras* (which is also the 2d pers. sing. of the Imperative); from which the following *four* Tenses, the Noun of Agency and the Present Participle, are formed:

TENSES OF THE ROOT.

1st.—The Aorist, *I may* or *can arrive;* formed by adding the terminations *am, ī, ad; em, ed, and;* to the root.

PERS.	SINGULAR.	PLURAL.
1.	رسم RAS*am,* "I may arrive."	رسیم RAS*em,* "We may arrive."
2.	رسي RAS*ī,* "Thou mayest arrive."	رسید RAS*ed,* "You may arrive."
3.	رسد RAS*ad,* "He may arrive."	رسند RAS*and,* "They may arrive."

2d.—THE PRESENT TENSE, *I am arriving*, or *I arrive;* formed by merely prefixing the Particle مِي *mī* to the Aorist; as,

PERS.	SINGULAR.	PLURAL.
1.	مِي رسم *mī*-RAS-*am*, "I am arriving."	مِي رسيم *mī*-RAS-*em*, "We are arriving."
2.	مِي رسي *mī*-RAS-*ī*, "Thou art arriving."	مِي رسيد *mī*-RAS-*ed*, "You are arriving."
3.	مِي رسد *mī*-RAS-ad, "He is arriving."	مِي رسند *mī*-RAS-*and*, "They are arriving."

3d.—THE SIMPLE FUTURE*, *I shall* or *may arrive;* formed by prefixing the Particle بِه or بِ *bi* to the Aorist.

1.	بِرسم *bi*-RAS-*am*, "I shall arrive."	بِرسيم *bi*-RAS-*em*, "We shall arrive."
2.	بِرسي *bi*-RAS-*ī*, "Thou wilt arrive."	بِرسيد *bi*-RAS-*ed*, "You will arrive."
3.	بِرسد *bi*-RAS-*ad*, "He will arrive."	بِرسند *bi*-RAS-*and*, "They will arrive."

4th.—THE IMPERATIVE, *Let me arrive.* The same as the Aorist, except in the 2d pers. sing., which consists of the mere root, without any termination.

1.	رسم RAS-*am*, "Let me arrive."	رسيم RAS*em*, "Let us arrive."
2.	رس RAS, "Arrive thou."	رسيد RAS*ed*, "Arrive you."
3.	رسد RAS-*ad*, "Let him arrive."	رسند RAS*and*, "Let them arrive."

* This Tense seems to differ very little from the Aorist, which, in its nature, frequently denotes futurity. The student, therefore, may consider it as a Simple Future, or as a modification of the Aorist; the latter being the opinion of all the Native Grammarians that we have had an opportunity of consulting.

From the root are also formed the Noun of Agency, by adding the termination ـَنْدَه *anda;* as, رَسَنْدَه RAS-*anda,* "the arriver": also the Present Participle, by adding ـَان; as, رسان RAS*ān,* "arriving."

The remaining parts of the verb come directly or indirectly from the Infinitive. The three following tenses (No. 5, 6, and 7) are formed directly by changing the final ن *n* of the Infinitive into the terminations of the Aorist; except in the 3d pers. sing., where no termination is added; together with other modifications which will be seen below:—thus, رَسِيدَن *rasīdan,* "to arrive," from which come directly—

5th.—PRETERITE OR INDEFINITE PAST, *I arrived.*

PERS.	SINGULAR.	PLURAL.
1.	رسيدم RASĪD-*am,* "I arrived."	رسيديم RASĪD-*em,* "We arrived."
2.	رسيدي RASĪD-*ī,* "Thou arrivedst."	رسيديد RASĪD-*ed,* "You arrived."
3.	رسيد RASĪD, "He arrived."	رسيدند RASĪD-*and,* "They arrived."

6th.—IMPERFECT, *I was arriving;* formed by prefixing the Particle مي *mī* to the Preterite.

1.	مي رسيدم *mī* RASĪD*am,* "I was arriving."	مي رسيديم *mī* RASĪD*em,* "We were arriving."
2.	مي رسيدي *mī* RASĪD*ī,* "Thou wast arriving."	مي رسيديد *mī* RASĪD*ed,* "You were arriving."
3.	مي رسيد *mī* RASĪD, "He was arriving."	مي رسيدند *mī* RASĪD*and,* "They were arriving."

7th.—The PAST POTENTIAL OR HABITUAL, *I might arrive,*

or *I used to arrive;* formed by adding ي *e* (*yae, majhūl*) to all the persons of the Preterite, except the 2d pers. sing., which is unchanged.

PERS.	SINGULAR.	PLURAL.
1.	رسيدمي RASĪD-*ame*, "I might arrive."	رسيديمي RASĪD-*eme*, "We might arrive."
2.	رسيدي RASĪD-*i*, "Thou mightest arrive."	رسيديدي RASĪD-*ede*, "You might arrive."
3.	رسيدي RASĪD-*e*, "He might arrive."	رسيدندي RASĪD-*ande*, "They might arrive."

8th.—COMPOUND FUTURE, *I will arrive;* formed by adding the Infinitive, generally deprived of its final syllable ـَن, to the Aorist (خواهم, &c.) of the verb خواستن *kh'āstan*, which signifies *to intend* or *wish*.

	SINGULAR	PLURAL
1.	خواهم رسيد *kh'āham* RASĪD, "I shall *or* will arrive."	خواهيم رسيد *kh'āhem* RASĪD, "We shall *or* will arrive."
2.	خواهي رسيد *kh'āhī* RASĪD, "Thou shalt *or* wilt arrive."	خواهيد رسيد *kh'āhed* RASĪD, "You shall *or* will arrive."
3.	خواهد رسيد *khāhad* RASĪD, "He shall *or* will arive."	خواهند رسيد *kh'āhand* RASĪD, "They shall *or* will arrive."

The three following tenses are compounded of the Preterite, Participle, and Auxiliaries. This Participle is regularly formed by changing the final ن *n* of the Infinitive into the obscure ه *h;* as from رسيدن *rasīdan*, "to arrive," comes رسيده *rasīdah*, "arrived" or "having arrived": hence,

9th.—The Perfect Tense, *I have arrived.*

PERS.	SINGULAR.		PLURAL.	
1.	رسيده ام	RASĪD*ah-am*, "I have arrived."	رسيده ايم	RASĪD*ah-em*, "We have arrived."
2.	رسيده اي or رسيده	RASĪD*ah-ī*, "Thou hast arrived."	رسيده ايد	RASĪD*ah-ed*, "You have arrived."
3.	رسيده است	RASĪD*ah-ast*, "He has arrived."	رسيده اند	RASĪD*ah-and*, "They have arrived."

10th.—Pluperfect Tense, *I had arrived.*

1.	رسيده بودم	RASĪD*ah būdam*, "I had arrived."	رسيده بوديم	RASĪD*ah būdem*, "We had arrived."
2.	رسيده بودي	RASĪD*ah būdī*, "Thou hadst arrived."	رسيده بوديد	RASĪD*ah būded*, "You had arrived."
3.	رسيده بود	RASĪD*ah būd*, "He had arrived."	رسيده بودند	RASĪD*ah būdand*, "They had arrived."

11th.—Future Perfect, *I shall have arrived.*

1.	رسيده باشم	RASĪD*ah bāsham*, "I shall have arrived."	رسيده باشيم	RASĪD*ah bāshem*, "We shall have arrived."
2.	رسيده باشي	RASĪD*ah bāshī*, "Thou shall have arrived."	رسيده باشيد	RASĪD*ah bāshed*, "You shall have arrived."
3.	رسيده باشد	RASĪD*ah bāshad*, "He shall have arrived."	رسيده باشند	RASĪD*ah bāshand*, "They shall have arrived."

36. In the preceding manner may be conjugated every verb in the Persian Language, provided one knows the Infinitive and the Root. The Infinitive is the part generally given in Dictionaries; and thence the Root may be readily ascertained, by a few simple rules:

GENERAL RULES.

1st, Every Infinitive ends in دن *dan* or تن *tan;* and the Imperative or Root is found by the rules which we are about to give. 2dly, The Aorist is formed by adding to the root the terminations *am, ī, ad; ēm, ēd, and.* 3dly, By dropping the final ن of the Infinitive, we have the 3d pers. sing. of the Preterite; and by adding the terminations above given, the rest of the Preterite is invariably formed. 4thly, The Perfect Participle is formed by changing the final ن of the Infinitive into ه imperceptible; and thence may be formed the Compound Tenses: hence it follows, that if the Infinitive and Imperative be known, the remaining parts of the verb are easily formed.

a. Infinitives in *dan* are preceded by the long vowels *ā,* (a few by the short *ă,*) *ī,* or *ū,* or by the consonants *r* and *n.* Those in *tan* are preceded by the strong consonants *kh, s, sh,* or *f*: hence the following special rules:

RULE I.

Infinitives in ادن—*ādan* and یدن— *īdan* reject these terminations for the Root; as, فرستادن *firistādan,* "to send," root فرست *firist,* "send thou;" so پرسیدن *pursidan,* "to ask," root پرس *purs,* "ask thou." The following verbs are anomalous:

INFINITIVE.	ROOT.	INFINITIVE.	ROOT.
آمادن "to prepare,"	آما	آفریدن "to create,"	آفرین
دادن "to give,"	ده	چیدن "to gather,"	چین
زادن "to be born,"	زا	دیدن "to see,"	بین
گادن "to generate,"	گا	شنیدن "to hear,"	شنو
گشادن "to open,"	گشا	گزیدي "to choose,"	گزین

To these may be added the following verbs in دن, preceded by the short vowel *ă*; there may be a few more such in the language, but their number is by no means great.

INFINITIVE.		ROOT.	INFINITIVE.		ROOT.
آژدن	"to sew," "pierce,"	آژ	زدن	"to strike,"	زن
آمدن	"to come,"	آ *or* آي	ستدن	"to take," "seize,"	ستان

RULE II.

Infinitives in ـُودن *ūdan* reject that termination, and substitute ـاي *āe* for the root; as, ستودن "to praise," ستاي. The exceptions are—

بودن	"to be *or* remain,"	بو *or* باش	زنودن	"to neigh," "howl,"	زنو
تنودن	"to draw,"	تنو	شدن	"to be *or* become,"	شو
درودن	"to reap,"	درو	شنودن	"to hear,"	شنو
			غنودن	"to slumber,"	غنو

The Infinitive شدن is a contraction of شودن or شويدن.

RULE III.

Infinitives in دن *dan*, preceded by د, ر, or ز inert, reject the termination دن for the root; as, كندن *kandan*, "to dig," كن *kan*; پروردن *parwardan*, "to cherish," پرور *parwar*; ازدن or آزدن *azdan*, "to sew," از or آز. The exceptions are—

آزردن	"to vex," "offend,"	آزار	شمردن	"to reckon,"	شمار
افشردن	"to press,"	افشار	فركندن	"to dig a canal,"	فركند
آوردن	"to bring,"	آور *or* آر	كردن	"to do," "make,"	كن
بردن	"to bear," "carry,"	بر	گندن	"to rot,"	گند
سپردن	"to entrust,"	سپار	مردن	"to die,"	مير

Several of the exceptions under Rules II. and III. have, at the same time, regular Infinitives ending in ـِيدن *īdan;* as, تَنَوِيدن, whence the regular root تَنَو; so, شُمارِيدن "to count," شُمار.

RULE IV.

Infinitives in تن *tan*, preceded by خ inert, reject تن, and change خ into ز for the root; as, انداختن "to throw," انداز. The following are exceptions:

INFINITIVE.		ROOT.	INFINITIVE.		ROOT.
آختن	"to draw a sword,"	آخ	شِناختن	"to know,"	شِناس
دوختن	"to milk,"	دوش	فروختن	"to sell,"	فروش
سختن	"to weigh,"	سنج	گُسیختن	"to split,"	گُسِل

RULE V.

Infinitives in تن, preceded by س inert, reject both the تن and س for the root; as, زِیستن "to live," زِي. To this rule the following are exceptions:

بستن	"to bind,"	بند	رُستن	"to grow,"	روي
پیوستن	"to mix," "unite,"	پیوند	شُستن	"to wash,"	شوي
جستن	"to leap,"	جه	شِکستن	"to break,"	شِکن
جُستن	"to seek,"	جوي	کاستن	"to lessen,"	کاه
خاستن	"to rise,"	خیز	گُسستن	"to break,"	گُسِل
خَواستن	"to wish,"	خواه	نِشاستن	"to cause to sit,"	نِشان
رستن	"to escape,"	ره	نِشستن	"to sit,"	نِشین

RULE VI.

Infinitives in تن, preceded by ش inert, reject تن, and change

ش into ر ; as, داشتن "to have *or* possess," دار. The following are exceptions:

INFINITIVE.		ROOT.	INFINITIVE.		ROOT.
آغاشتن	"to accumulate,"	آغاش	گشتن	"to become," "turn,"	گرد
آغوشتن	"to embrace,"	آغوش	نوشتن	"to write,"	نویس
افراشتن	"to exalt,"	افراز	هشتن	"to quit,"	هش *or* هل

RULE VII.

Infinitives in تن, preceded by ف inert, generally reject تن, and change ف into ب; as, تافتن "to shine," "twist," &c. تاب; but in some verbs the ف remains unchanged in the root; as, بافتن "to weave," باف. The following are exceptions:

پذیرفتن	"to accept,"	پذیر	شنفتن	"to hear,"	شنو
خفتن	"to sleep,"	خسپ	کافتن	"to dig," "cleave,"	کاو
رفتن	"to go,"	رو	گرفتن	"to take,"	گیر
سفتن	"to bore,"	سنب	گفتن	"to say,"	گوي

Sometimes the short vowel preceding the termination of the Infinitive is lengthened in the root; as, رفتن "to sweep," روب.

37. Let the Student carefully commit to memory the preceding Rules, together with their exceptions; after which he will have no difficulty in conjugating any Persian Verb of ordinary occurrence. Let it be remembered, at the same time, that there is not, strictly speaking, any *Irregular Verb* in this language. For instance, the verbs بین دیدن "to see," and کن کردن "to do," are

no more irregular than the corresponding Latin Verbs *video, vidi, visum;* and *ago, egi, actum;* for in both languages the various tenses &c. are formed from their respective sources or principal parts, according to general rules. It may be observed, also, that most of the roots given as exceptions to the preceding rules have regular Infinitives in *īdan* still in use; in fact, we ought in strictness to consider the Infinitives as anomalous, and the roots regular. Thus, هِشْتَن "to quit," "dismiss," has for its root هِل or هِش, which really come from the regular Infinitive هِلِيدَن or هِشِيدَن, still in use; whilst هِشْتَن itself is a very natural contraction of هِشِيدَن into هِشْدَن, and ultimately هِشتَن.

As a specimen of an anomalous Verb, (if we may so call it) we here subjoin the verb زدن *zadan,* "to strike," root زن *zan,* which, to save room, we shall give in the Roman character.*

1st.—TENSES OF THE ROOT.

	SINGULAR.			PLURAL.		
Aorist	*zan-am*	*ī*	*ad*	*em*	*ed*	*and*
Present	*mī-zan-am*	*ī*	*ad*	*em*	*ed*	*and*
Second Future,	*bi-zan-am*	*ī*	*ad*	*em*	*ed*	*and*
Imperative . . .	*zanam*	*zan*	*zan-ad*	*em*	*ed*	*and*

Agent and Participle Active, { *zanandah* "the striker," *zanān* "striking."

* It will be a useful exercise for the Student to write out this verb at full length in the Persian character; to which he may add, *dīdan,* root *bīn* "to see," and *shudan,* root *shav* "to be," or "become."

2d.—TENSES OF THE INFINITIVE.

	SINGULAR.			PLURAL.		
Preterite	*zadam*	*zadī*	*zad*	*zad-em*	*-ed*	*-and*
Imperfect .	*mī-zadam*	—	—	—	—	—
Past Potential,	*zadame*	*zadī*	*zade*	*zad-eme*	*-ede*	*-ande*
Comp. Future,	*kh'āham zad, kh'āhī zad, kh'āhad zad,* &c.					
Pret. Participle,	*zadah* "stricken," "struck," "having struck."					
Perfect	*zadah-am*	*-ī*	*-ast*	*-em*	*-ed*	*-and*
Pluperfect . . .	*zadahbūdam*	*būdī*	*būd*	*būd-em*	*-ed*	*-and*
Future Perfect,	*zadah bāsh-am*	*-ī*	*-ad*	*-em*	*-ed*	*-and*

To this we may add another useful verb of frequent occurrence, شُدن *shudan,* "to be," "to go," "to become," root شَو *shav.*

Aorist	*shav-am*	*ī*	*ad*	*em*	*ed*	*and*
Present	*mī-shav-am*	—	—	—	—	—
Second Future,	*bi-shav-am*	—	—	—	—	—
Imperative . ,	*shavam,*	*shav*	*shav-ad*	—	—	—
Agent and Part.	*shavandah* and *shavān,* "being," or "becoming."					
Preterite . . .	*shud-am*	*shudī*	*shud,* &c.			
Imperfect . . .	*mī-shud-am,* &c.					
Past Potential,	*shudame*	*shudī*	*shude,* &c.			
Comp. Future,	*kh'āham shud, khahī shud,* &c.					
Pret. Participle,	*shudah,* "been," or "become."					
Perfect	*shudah am, shudah ī, shudah ast,* &c.					
Pluperfect . . .	*shudah būdam, shadah budī, shudah būd,* &c.					
Future Perfect,	*shudah basham, shudah bashī, shudah bashad,* &c.					

PASSIVE VOICE.

38. The Passive Voice is regularly formed by prefixing the Preterite Participle to the various tenses of the verb شُدن, which we have just exemplified. Thus, the Passive of the verb زدن is formed as follows:

PRESENT.

SINGULAR.	PLURAL.
زده شَوَم "I may be struck."	زده شَوِيم "We may be struck."
زده شَوِي "Thou mayest be struck."	زده شَوِيد "You may be struck."
زده شَوَد "He may be struck."	زده شَوَنْد "They may be struck."

PRETERITE.

زده شُدم "I was struck."	زده شُدِيم "We were struck."
زده شُدِي "Thou wast struck."	زده شُدِيد "You were struck."
زده شُد "He was struck."	زده شُدَنْد "They were struck."

It would be superfluous to add more of the Passive Voice, in the formation of which the Persian very much resembles our own language.

CAUSAL VERBS.

39. These are formed by adding the termination ـَانِيدن *ānīdan*, or, contracted, ـَانْدن *āndan*, to the root of the primitive verb; thus, جسْتن, root جه "to leap"; from which جهانِيدن "to cause to leap"; so رسِيدن, root رس "to arrive"; رسانِيدن or رساندن "to cause to arrive," "to send." All Causal Verbs form their roots according to Rules I. and III.

a. There are a few other compound tenses, or rather modes of expression, besides those given in the paradigm of رسِيدن (p. 35 &c.), which will be treated of in the Syntax. It will be proper to add here, that, according to Dr. Lumsden, whose authority we consider decisive on this point (owing to his frequent intercourse with learned Natives), "the sound of the letter ي in the terminations ـيم and

يد— (1st and 2d persons plur.) of all the tenses is what is called *majhūl*. The final ي added to the Preterite in forming the Potential, or continuative past time, is *majhūl* in the 1st and 3d pers. singular, and in the 3d pers. plural. In all the tenses the final ي (or *hamza* when substituted), in the 2d pers. sing., is *ma'rūf*." This remark is the more essential, as many Natives of Persia (at least the uneducated) deny the existence, in their language, of the sound represented by و and ي *majhūl*, which they always pronounce like و and ي *ma'rūf;* i. e. instead of روز *roz*, "a day," they say *rūz ;* and instead of بيل *bel*, "a spade," they say *bīl*. Dr. Lumsden states, however, "that the distinction is recognised in every Lexicon, and will not be controverted by a well-educated Persian. It ought therefore to be carefully retained by those who are desirous of acquiring an accurate and classical pronunciation."—Lumsden's Pers. Gram. vol. I. p. 72.

b. The verbal terminations of the Perfect Tense (p. 39) are frequently used with Substantives, Adjectives, and Participles, to denote simple affirmation or assertion. In such cases, the initial ا of the terminations is omitted, and the vowel which it forms becomes united with the last consonant of the word preceding ; thus,

SINGULAR.		PLURAL.	
من شاگردم	"I am a scholar."	ما شاگردانيم	"We are scholars."
تُو چاكرِي	"Thou art a servant."	شُما چاكرانيد	"You are servants."
او عاقلست	"He is sensible."	ايشان دزدانند	"They are thieves."

But if the preceding word ends in the weak ه, the ا is retained in the verbal terminations ; as, بندہ ام "I am a slave"; تُو ديوانه اي or تُو ديوانهٔ "Thou art mad"; فرِشته است "He (she *or* it) is an angel." If the preceding word ends in the vowels ا or و, the letter ي is inserted, to prevent a hiatus between these and the verbal terminations ; as, بينايم "I am seeing"; دانائي "Thou art wise"; خوبرويست and (contracted) خوبروست "He *or* she is fair-faced."

c. Somewhat akin to the preceding terminations is another fragment of a verb denoting "to be," "to exist," used under the form of a Preterite, but generally with the sense of a Present Tense; as,

SINGULAR.		PLURAL.	
هستم	"I am *or* exist."	هستیم	"We are *or* exist."
هستي	"Thou art *or* existest."	هستید	"You are *or* exist."
هست	"He is *or* exists."	هستند	"They are *or* exist."

This verb is also used as an Auxiliary in forming a Preter-Perfect Tense, by being joined to the Preterite Participle; in which case both the final ة of the Participle and the initial ه of the Auxiliary are rejected; as, شُنیدستم "I have heard"; دیدستي "Thou hast seen"; پرسیدست "He has asked." This form of the Preter-Perfect is frequently used in poetry, simply because it may happen to suit the poet's metre. It does not seem to differ in signification from the ordinary form given in page 39.

OF NEGATIVE AND PROHIBITIVE VERBS.

40. A Verb is rendered negative by prefixing the Particle نه (or نَ) *na*, "not"; as, نه رسید or نرسید "He did not arrive." With the Imperative, the Particle مه (or مَ) *ma* is employed in like manner, to express prohibition; as, مه پرس or مپرس "Ask not"; so مباد or مبادا "Let it not be," frequently used in the sense of "God forbid."

a. When the Particles بِ, نَ, or مَ are prefixed to a verb beginning with ا, not marked by the symbol ـَـ (§. 17.), the letter ي is inserted to prevent a hiatus; the ا is then omitted, and its vowel transferred to the inserted ي; thus, انداخت *andākht*, "He threw"; نَيَنداخت *nayandākht*, "He did not throw": Aorist, اُفتم *uftam*, "I may fall"; Future, بِيُفتم *biyuftam*, "I shall fall": انگار

"consider"; مَيَنْگار "consider not." If the verb begins with آ, the ا remains, but the *madda* ـٓ is rejected; thus, آرَد "He may bring"; بِيارد "He will bring"; آر "Bring thou"; مَيَار "Do not bring"; but this, in reality, is in strict conformity with the general rule; for آر is equivalent to أار: hence, in prefixing the particles along with the letter ي, the first ا is rejected, as we stated at the outset.* Finally, the negative نه, in verse, frequently unites with the following آ, without the intervention of the ي; as, نامد, for نَيَامد, "He came not."

b. The substantive verb هستم is rendered negative by changing the initial ه into ي, and prefixing نِ; thus,

SINGULAR.		PLURAL.	
نِيستم	"I am not."	نِيستيم	"We are not."
نِيستي	"Thou art not."	نِيستيد	"You are not."
نِيست	"He, &c. is not."	نِيستند	"They are not."

To denote simple negation, the verbal terminations noticed §. 39. *b.* are subjoined to the particle نه, as follows:

نَيَم	"I am not."	نَئِيم	"We are not."
نئي *or* نهٔ	"Thou art not."	نَئِيد	"You are not."
نِيست	"He &c. is not."	نَيَند	"They are not."

---

* On a similar principle the initial ا is omitted in the pronouns اِين "this," and آن (properly أان) "that," when they are closely connected with the preceding word; as, بِرِين "on this," instead of بر اِين; so, دران "in that," for در آن. I have reason to believe that this principle is of a very extensive application; but the discussion to which it would lead would be here out of place.

SECTION IV.

ON THE INDECLINABLE PARTS OF SPEECH. — CARDINAL NUMBERS. — DERIVATION AND COMPOSITION OF WORDS.

ADVERBS.

41. The Persian Language offers no peculiarity on the score of Adverbs, except its extreme simplicity: hence it would be superfluous to occupy our pages with a dry list of words, which more properly belong to the Vocabulary. We may briefly mention, that, in this language, adverbs are formed, or rather adopted, as follows:

a. 1st, *Substantives* with or without a preposition; as, گاهي "one, *or* any time"; نام "by name"; شب و روز "night and day"; به خوبي "perfectly"; درنهان "secretly." 2dly, Adjectives without undergoing any change; as, خوب "well"; سخت "severely," &c. In fact, all adjectives may be used adverbially, if necessary, as is frequently the case in German, and sometimes in English; thus, "the eagle soars high"; "the fish swims deep." 3dly, Adjective or Interrogative Pronouns with Substantives; as, اينجا "here," آنجا "there"; كجا "where?" چگونه "how?" كدام طرف "whither?" &c. These again may be preceded by a preposition; as, از اينجا "hence"; درآنجا "there." Lastly, there are some Arabic nouns in the Accusative Case used adverbially in Persian; as, حالاً "presently"; قصداً "purposely."

PREPOSITIONS.

42. The simple Prepositions in this language are very few, probably not more than seven or eight in number. These are, از (in poetry frequently contracted into زِ) "from," "by"; با "with (in company with)"; بر and ابر "on," "upon"; به or بِ "in," "by," "to"; بي "without (deprived of)"; تا "up to," "as far as"; جُز "except," "besides"; در "in." In their application they are placed before the simple or nominative forms both of nouns and pronouns; as, درشهر "in the city"; برمن "on me"; با تو "with thee"; جُزايشان "except them."

a. The rest of the prepositions are, strictly speaking, substantives or adjectives, having one of the simple particles above mentioned expressed or understood. Such of them as are substantives require the *izāfat*, or sign of the genitive case, between them and the noun which they govern; as, زيرِزمين "under the ground"; بالاي درخت "above the tree (*i.e.* on the top of the tree)"; به نزديكِ شهر "near the city," literally, "to, or in the vicinity of the city." Some of them may be viewed as adjectives denoting comparison; as, پيش ازمن (for پيشتر ازمن) "before me"; پس از آن "after that." All these compound prepositions may of course be used adverbially when occasion requires, as is the case in English; thus, بيرون رفت "he went out"; پيش آمد "he came forward"; پس ماند "he remained behind."

CONJUNCTIONS.

43. Primitive Conjunctions, like the simple Prepositions, are not numerous. The following are of frequent

occurrence:—اگر, گر "if"; بلکه "but," "on the contrary"; تا "whilst," "until"; چون, چو "when," "as"; که, چه "that," "for," "as"; لیکن "but"; نیز "also"; و "and" (pronounced *wa,* and sometimes *o*); هم "even," "also"; یا "or," "either."

a. There are also, as might be expected, many compound phrases employed in this language as conjunctions; as, حال آن که "whereas," "inasmuch as"; پیش ازانکه "before that (*antequam*); so, بعد ازانکه "after that (*posteaquam*)."

INTERJECTIONS.

44. In Persian, as in other languages, Interjections consist partly of adventitious sounds denoting the passions and emotions of the speaker; as, آه "ah!" اي "O!" &c.; and partly of substantives expressive of pain or pleasure, used elliptically, or in the vocative case; as, افسوس "Alas!" دریغ or دریغا "Oh, unfortunate!" To say more about this part of speech (if it may be so called) would be uselessly encroaching on the department of the Vocabulary.

NUMERALS.

45. In the following Table we shall give the leading Cardinal Numbers, together with the corresponding Arabian and European figures. It is needless to say that the whole system is extremely simple, and very similar to what we have in English.

CARDINAL NUMBERS.

یک	١	1	بِیسْتُ و یک	٢١	21
دُو	٢	2	بِیسْتُ و دُو	٢٢	22
سِه	٣	3	سِی	٣٠	30
چهار	۴	4	چِهل	۴٠	40
پنْج	۵	5	پنْجاه	۵٠	50
شش	۶	6	شسْت	۶٠	60
هفْت	٧	7	هَفْتاد	٧٠	70
هشْت	٨	8	هشْتاد	٨٠	80
نُه	٩	9	نَوَد	٩٠	90
ده	١٠	10	صد	١٠٠	100
یازْده	١١	11	صدُ و یک	١٠١	101
دُوَازْده	١٢	12	دُوصد	٢٠٠	200
سِیزْده	١٣	13	سِصد	٣٠٠	300
چهارْده	١۴	14	چهارْصد	۴٠٠	400
پانْزْده	١۵	15	پانْصد	۵٠٠	500
شانْزْده	١۶	16	ششْصد	۶٠٠	600
هفْده	١٧	17	هفْتْصد	٧٠٠	700
هشْده	١٨	18	هشْتْصد	٨٠٠	800
نُوزْده	١٩	19	نُهْصد	٩٠٠	900
بِیسْت	٢٠	20	هَزار	١٠٠٠	1000

The formation of the Ordinal Numbers will be treated of under the head of Derivative Adjectives.

a. The above figures or numeric cyphers, now used by the Arabs and Persians, are read like ours, from left to right; thus, the year of our æra 1845 is ١٨٤٥; so the corresponding year of the Hijra 1261 is ١٢٦١. It is generally admitted, even by the Arabs themselves, that the decimal scale of notation was invented in India, and thence brought to Arabia. By the Arabs it was introduced into Europe through Spain; and hence the system goes under the name of the Arabian Notation. At first sight it would appear to be at variance with the Arabian mode of reading (from right to left); but this is not really the case, as the Arabs do read the numbers from right to left. Thus, instead of saying, "In the year of the Hijra (١٢٦١) One thousand two hundred and sixty-one," the Arabs say, "In the year of the Hijra, One and sixty and two hundred and one thousand," or "two hundred after the thousand."

b. The Mussulmāns reckon by lunar time in all their transactions, commencing from the day on which Muhammad departed from Mecca; which, according to the best accounts, took place on Friday, the 16th of July (18th, new style), A.D. 622. Their year consists of 12 lunations, amounting to 354 days and 9 hours, very nearly: hence their New-year's Day will happen every year about eleven days earlier than in the preceding year. It follows, then, that there must be some difficulty in finding the exact day of the Christian æra which corresponds to any given Mussulmān date. The following rule will suffice for finding the number of solar or Christian years elapsed since any given Mussulmān date:—"Subtract the given year of the Hijra from the current year of the same, and from the remainder deduct *three per cent*; then you will have the number of solar or Christian years elapsed." Thus, we see a valuable manuscript of a Persian Poem (suppose the Hadīka of Sanāyī), written A.H. 681. We subtract this from the present year of the Hijra, 1260; there remains 579: from this we deduct 3 *per cent*, or one year for every 33; the result is 562, the real age of the MS. in Solar years: hence it must have been written about

A.D. 1282. This simple rule is founded on the fact, that 100 lunar years are very nearly equal to 97 solar years, there being only about eight days of difference. A more accurate proportion would be 101 lunar to 98 solar years; but this would lead to a less convenient rule for practical use.

DERIVATION OF WORDS.

46. In Persian, the derivation of one word from another is effected by means of certain terminations, in a manner similar to that which prevails in most of the European languages. The words so derived are chiefly substantives and adjectives, together with a few verbs and adverbs, all of which we shall notice in their order.

1st.—OF SUBSTANTIVES.

a. Substantives denoting an agent or performer are derived from other substantives by adding the terminations بان or وان, گار or گر; as, from در "a door," دربان or دروان "a door-keeper"; from خدمت "service," خدمتگار "a servant *or* attendant"; so, from زر "gold," زرگر "a goldsmith, *or* worker in gold." In modern Persian, the termination چي (apparently from the Turkish) is sometimes met with; as, from بندوق "a musket," بندوقچي "a musketeer."

b. Names relating to the place of any thing are formed by adding ستان, بار, دان, زار, and لاخ; as, شيرستان "a place abounding with lions," from شير "a lion"; شمع دان "a candlestick," from شمع "a candle or lamp"; گلزار "a rose-bed," from گل "a rose or flower"; so, from سنگ "a stone," سنگلاخ "a place abounding with stones."

c. Diminutives are formed by adding ـك for names of animals;

زه (sometimes يزه) for inanimate beings; and چه, or ـِيچه, applicable to any nouns; thus, مردك "a little man," from مرد "a man"; دانزه "a small grain," from دانه "a grain"; دريچه "a little door *or* window," from در "a door."

d. An Abstract Noun may be formed from any adjective, simple or compound, by the addition of ـِي *ma'rūf;* as, نيكي "goodness," from نيك "good;" جهان داري "the possessing of the world," "royalty," from جهان دار "world-possessing," an epithet applied to monarchs. By adding ـِي to appellative nouns an abstract will be formed, denoting the state or profession indicated by the noun; as, بادشاهي "sovereignty," from بادشاه "a king;" سوداگري "traffic," from سوداگر "a merchant." If the primitive word should end in the weak ه, the ه is suppressed, and the letter گ inserted before adding the termination ي; as, آزرده "sad," آزردگي "sadness;" so, بنده "slave," بندگي "slavery."

e. Verbal Nouns are formed by changing the final syllable ـَن *an* of the Infinitive into ـَار; as, ديدن "to see," ديدار "seeing," "a sight." The Infinitive itself is frequently used as a general verbal noun, like our words in *ing*; as, آمدنِ رستم "the coming of Rustam." In a few phrases the final ـَن of the Infinitive is rejected; as, آمد وشد "coming and going;" so, خريد و فروخت "buying and selling," "traffic." Another class of verbal nouns is formed from the root by adding ـِي or ـِش; as, گوي "speaking," "conversation," from گو, the root of گفتن "to speak"; so, آفرينش "creation," from افرين, the root of افريدن "to create." The noun denoting the agent of a verb is formed (as already stated, page 37) by adding the termination ـَنده to the root; as, آفرينند‌ه "the Creator": and if the root ends with the long vowels *ā* or *ō*, the letter ي is inserted between it and the termination; as, گوينده "the speaker."

2d.—OF ADJECTIVES.

f. Adjectives denoting possession, &c. are formed by adding to nouns the terminations ا, سار, گِین, مَنْد, وار, ور or ـُور, and ـِین; as, from the root دان "know," دانا "learned"; شرمسار "bashful," from شَرم "shame"; غمگِین "sorrowful," from غم "sorrow"; دولتمَنْد "wealthy"; اُمیدوار "hopeful," from اُمید "hope"; جانْور "possessed of life," "an animal," from جان "life," "soul"; رنجور "sorrowful," from رنْج "sorrow"; زرِین "golden," from زر "gold."

g. The terminations آسا, سا, سار, and وَش, added to nouns, form adjectives denoting similitude"; فام and گُون denote resemblance in colour; as, مُشك آسا "like musk"; خاكسار "like dust," "humble"; مَهْوَش "like the moon"; لعل‌فام "ruby-coloured"; لاله گُون "of the colour of tulip."

h. A large class of adjectives, which may be termed gentile, patronymic, or relàtive, is formed from substantives, by adding the termination ـِي; thus, from اِیران "Persia," اِیرانِي "Persian"; from هِنْد "India," هِنْدِي "Indian"; from the city, شِیراز, comes شِیرازِي "of, *or* belonging to Shīrāz"; so, from the substantives شَهْر "a city," جَنْگل "a forest," بَحْر "the sea," are formed the adjectives شَهْرِي, جَنْگلِي, بَحْرِي. This termination is of extensive use in the formation of both substantives and adjectives.

i. The terminations ـَانه and (sometimes) وار, added to nouns form adjectives, denoting general or natural resemblance: hence *fitness* or *worthiness,* of the original noun; as, مرْدانه "manful," "worthy of a man"; دیوانه "demoniac," "worthy of a (دیو) demon"; شاهْوار "princely, *or* fit for a prince."

j. By adding the termination ـُم to the cardinal numbers, we form the corresponding ordinal; thus, هفْتُم "the seventh," from

هفت "seven." When more words than one are required to express the ordinal number, the ـُم is added to the last only; as, بیست و هفتم, "the twenty-seventh." The word expressing the first of the ordinals, نُخُستین, is an exception: the Arabic word اوّل is also frequently used; as, بابِ اوّل "Book *or* Section the First"; but these words are not used, except for the *first* only. In the case of a number expressed by two or more numerals, of which the last is unity, the ordinal is formed by adding ـُم to the یك; as, بیست و یکم "the twenty-first." The ordinals *second* and *third* may be دویم, سِیُم or دُوم, سِیوم; the rest follow the rule.

3d.—OF VERBS.

k. The principal derivative verbs in Persian are those called Causal, already mentioned (§. 39). A few verbs are derived from Arabic roots by adding ـِیدن; as, طلبِیدن "to seek, *or* send for"; فهمیدن "to understand"; from the Arabic roots طلب and فهم, of the same signification.

4th.—OF ADVERBS.

l. We have already stated that adverbs in Persian have nothing peculiar in their formation, most adjectives being used as adverbs when occasion requires. This remark applies particularly to adjectives in ـانَه and وار (*i*); which, when they denote manner, as is often the case, may be considered as adverbs; as, پیادہ وار "in the manner of a pedestrian, *or* pawn at chess"; عاقِلانه "wisely"; دلیرانه "bravely."

COMPOSITION OF WORDS.

47. The Persian Language abounds with compound words, consisting principally of Substantives and Adjectives, in the formation of which it bears a considerable resemblance to the English and German. We might even say, that, in this respect, it equals or surpasses the Sanskrit and Greek; but the comparison would not be quite correct, as the Persian is void of inflections, and consequently its compounds, though numerous, are not so marked as in the ancient tongues. We shall here endeavour to describe the mode of forming the more useful compounds of the language, in the same order as the preceding paragraph on Derivative Words.

SUBSTANTIVES.

a. A numerous class of Compound Substantives is formed by the juxta-position of two other nouns, in the reverse order of the genitive case, the sign of the *izāfat* being rejected; as, باورچي خانه "cook-house, *or* kitchen," from باورچي "cook," and خانه "a house." This is, in fact, equivalent to خانهٔ باورچي "the house of the cook," with the order of the words reversed; so, رزم گاه "the battle field," from رزم "contest," and گاه "a place": in like manner, جهان پناه "the asylum of the world, *i.e.* the royal personage," from جهان "the world," and پناه "refuge"; so, روزنامه "a day-book," خرد نامه "the book of wisdom," &c. Compounds of this kind are extremely common in English and German, more so, indeed, than in Persian: witness such words as London Bridge, Custom House, Thames Tunnel, and thousands besides.

b. There is a class of Verbal Nouns, not very numerous, consisting, 1st, of two contracted infinitives, connected with the conjunction و; as, گفت وشنود "conversation," literally, "speaking and hearing"; آمد ورفت "coming and going," "intercourse." 2dly, A contracted infinitive, with the corresponding root; as, جست وجو "searching"; گفت وگو "conversation." The conjunction

و in such cases is occasionally omitted; as, گُفت گو, آمد شد, the same as آمد وشد, &c.

c. There are a few compounds similar to the preceding, consisting of two substantives, sometimes of the same, and sometimes of different signification; as, مرز و بوم or مرز و کشور "an empire *or* kingdom," literally, "boundary and region"; so, آب وهوا "climate," literally, "water and air"; نشو و نما "rearing *or* bringing up (a plant or animal)." In these, also, the conjunction و may be omitted; as, مرزبوم, نشو نما, &c.

d. An infinitive or verbal noun, preceded by the particle نا, is rendered negative; as, نا شنودن the "non-hearing." The difference between the use of the نا and نه will be treated of in the Syntax.

e. A few substantives are compounded of a numeral and another substantive; as, چارپاي "a quadruped"; سه پهر "the afternoon being the third *pahr* or watch of the day"; so the days of the week, يك شنبه "Sunday," دو شنبه "Monday," سه شنبه "Tuesday," &c. We may add, with regard to compound substantives in general, that they confer great strength and expressiveness on a language. We no longer view the ideas represented by each member of the compound separately, but we conceive the two blended together into one new idea. Thus, خانهٔ باورچي "the house of the cook," and باورچي خانه, though of nearly the same import, yet convey very different ideas to the mind; and the same may be said of all others.

ADJECTIVES, OR EPITHETS.

f. In these the Persian Language is particularly rich, every writer using them more or less, according to his own pleasure. A very numerous class of epithets is formed by the union of two substantives; as, لاله رُخ "having cheeks like the tulip"; پري رُوي "having the face of a fairy"; سنگ دل "having a heart like stone";

شکرلب "having lips (sweet) as sugar." It would be needless to extend the list; we may merely observe that the idea conveyed by compounds of this sort is, that the person to whom the epithet is applicable is possessed of the object expressed in the second member of the compound, in a degree equal to, or resembling, the first. In English we have many instances, in the more familiar style, of this kind of compound; as, "iron-hearted," "bull-headed," "lynx-eyed," &c.

g. Another numerous class, similar to the preceding, is formed by prefixing an adjective to a substantive; as, خُوب رُوي "having a fair face"; پاك راي "of pure intention"; تنگ دِل "distressed in heart"; زرین قلم "of a golden pen," an epithet applied to Mulla Muhammad Husain Kashmīrī*, the finest writer of the Ta'lik hand at the munificent Court of Akbar, and in all probability the finest that ever lived. The idea conveyed by these compounds is, that the person to whom they apply possesses the object expressed in the second member of the compound, in the state or manner indicated by the first. We have many such compounds in English, used in familiar conversation, and Newspaper style, such as "clear-sighted," "long-headed," "sharp-witted," "hard-hearted," &c.

h. Perhaps the most numerous class of the epithets is that composed of verbal roots joined to substantives or adjectives; as, عالم گیر "world-subduing"; فتنه انگیز "strife-exciting"; جان آسا "giving rest to the soul"; دِل ستان "ravishing the heart"; سُبُك رَو "moving lightly." Most Grammarians consider the verbal roots in such compounds as contractions of the present participle in

* It is impossible to imagine any thing more beautiful of its kind than the penmanship of Mulla Husain. I happen to possess a manuscript of the Bustān of Sa'di, written by him; and assuredly the perusal of a page thereof makes one view all other fine manuscripts as downright deformity. Mulla Husain was among penmen what Paganini was among fiddlers.

سَان or سَا. We do, indeed, sometimes find the real participle in use; as, دِل آوران "intrepid," literally, "heart-bearing (German, *herzhaft*)"; so, سَرْو رَوَان "moving *or* waving like a cypress"; but the occurrence of such phrases is very rare, compared with those ending in the verbal root. The Greek Language has numerous compounds of the same kind, in substance similar to the Persian, such as ἐργολάβος "one who undertakes a work," and ἱπποτρόφος "one who rears horses," where we have the noun and verbal root in the simple state, or crude form, with the termination ος superadded; so that the agreement between the Greek and Persian compound is complete, the latter language having no termination to add. Hence there is no solid reason for calling the verbal roots, in Persian compounds, *participles;* while, on the contrary, the use of the term is objectionable, as it misleads the student. Compound epithets of a similar kind are frequently used by our best English Poets; such as, "the night-tripping fairy"; "the cloud-compelling Jove"; "the temple-haunting martlet."

i. Another class of epithets is compounded of a substantive and a past participle; as, جهان دِيده "experienced," "one who has seen the world"; جَنْگ آزمُوده "one who has been tried in battle," *i.e.* "trained to war"; so, غم خُورْده "one who has felt sorrow"; دام نِهاده "one who has laid a snare"; مِحْنت كشيده "one who has endured affliction."

k. There is an extensive class of adjectives formed by prefixing the particles با "with, *or* possessed of"; and بي "without, *or* deprived of," to substantives; as, با مال "rich," "possessed of wealth"; با رامش "cheerful, *or* joyous," an epithet applied to the planet Venus; so, بي دِل "heartless, *or* disconsolate"; بي اِنْصاف "unjust"; بي نِياز "without need," "He who is above all assistance," an epithet applied to the Almighty.

l. The particles كم and هم, prefixed to nouns and verbal roots, form a considerable class of epithets. كم literally denotes "little"; but in composition it seems almost to convey the idea of "nothing, *or* negation"; as, كم زور "of little strength"; كم خِرد "of little sense," "stupid"; كم خُور "eating little," "abstemious"; كم ياب "improcurable." The particle هم denotes "equality, *or* association"; and, like the preceding, is compounded with nouns or verbal roots. Its effect is the same as the Greek ἁμα, or the Latin *con*; as, هم راه "a fellow-traveller, *or* one who goes on the same road," the same as ακολουθος (from ἁμα and κελευθος); so, هم عُمر "of the same age," "coeval"; هم نِشِين "intimate," "sitting together"; هم باز "a playfellow." We may add, in conclusion, that almost all the compounds, of the species described in paragraphs *f*, *g*, *h*, *i*, *k*, and *l*, may occur either as substantives or adjectives; hence they may be appropriately classed under the term Epithets or Compound Epithets.

m. The particle نا, prefixed to an adjective, simple or compound, renders it negative; as, نا پاك "impure," from پاك "pure"; so, from پاك راي "of pure, *or* sincere intention," comes نا پاك راي "of wicked intention." It is also prefixed to verbal roots and participles; as, نا دان "ignorant,", نا ستُوده "not commended," "disreputable." Sometimes it is prefixed to substantives; as, ناكام "not according to one's desire," perhaps elliptically for نا بكام; for we meet with ناكار and نابكار "worthless," still in use. The particle نا has the same effect in Persian as the privative *a* of the Sanskrit and Greek, the *in* of the Latin, and the *un* of the English and German. Finally, in all the preceding compounds we have preserved the component parts separate, though in manuscripts they may be united or not, at the option of the writer.

VERBS.

n. Persian Verbs, like those of the Sanskrit, Greek, &c., may be compounded with a preposition; as, درآمدن "to come in";

برخاستن "to rise up." Adverbs may also be prefixed in like manner; as, فرو نشستن "to sit down"; بالا پريدن "to soar upwards"; but in such phrases there is hardly any peculiarity deserving the name of a compound.

o. The verbs كَرْدن, ساختن, فرمودن, and نمودن are frequently used with substantives or adjectives, in the general sense of "making"; as, حُكم كردن "to make an order," "to command"; خُشنود ساختن "to make content," "to satisfy"; اِلتفات نمودن "to attend," "to notice"; مُطالعه فرمودن "to peruse (a letter)." The verbs داشتن and زدن are occasionally used in the same sense; as, طلب داشتن "to make search"; رائي زدن "to express an opinion." The verbs خوردن and ديدن are used in the sense of "to suffer," "to experience"; as, غم خوردن "to grieve"; مِحنت ديدن "to suffer affliction." In this general acceptation, the verb ديدن "to see" occasionally encroaches on some of the other senses; as, بوئي ديدن "to smell," literally, "to see *or* experience fragrance."

p. A knowledge of the Persian compounds will be absolutely necessary, in order to peruse with advantage the finest productions of the language. The poets in general make frequent use of such terms; and several grave historians indulge freely in the practice. In the version of Pilpay's Fables, entitled, The Anvāri Suhaili, by Husain Vaiz, there are at least as many compounds as sentences; and the same may be said of the Tales of Ināyat Ullah, called, The Bahār i Dānish: but the perfection of the system will be found in the commencement of a Persian epistle, wherein it is a point of etiquette to employ a great number of fine-sounding words, that mean nothing. The *business* part of the Letter is generally disposed of in a few lines, at the conclusion.

SECTION V.

ON SYNTAX.

ANALYSIS OF SENTENCES.

48. In the preceding Sections we have treated of the letters, syllables, and words of the Persian Language. We now come to the most important part of the subject—the construction of sentences, or, in other words, the rules for speaking and writing the language correctly. We have hitherto taken for granted that the Student is acquainted with the ordinary terms of Grammar, and is able to distinguish the various parts of speech (common to all languages) from one another. It is probable, however, that he may not have turned his attention to the analysis of sentences, which ought to form a preliminary step to the Syntax of every foreign tongue. On this account, we request his attention to the following general, or rather universal principles of language, an acquaintance with which will enable him to comprehend more fully some of the rules which we are about to state.

a. A simple sentence consists of three parts; viz. a nominative, or agent; a verb; and an attribute, or complement; as, "Fire is hot"; "Fire consumes wood." In the first sentence, *fire* is the nominative, or subject of affirmation; *hot* is the attribute, or that which is affirmed of the subject, *fire;* and the verb *is* serves to express the affirmation. Again, in the sentence "Fire consumes wood," *fire* is the nominative, or agent, *consumes* is the verb, and *wood* is the *object*. It appears, then, that the shortest sentence must consist of three words, expressed or understood; and it will be found that the longest is always reducible to three distinct parts, which may be considered as so many compound words. For example: "The scorching fire of the thunder-cloud utterly consumes the tall and verdant trees of the forest." In this sentence, the words *fire*, *consumes*, and *trees*, are qualified or restricted by particular circumstances: still, the complex term, "The scorching fire of the thunder-cloud" is the nominative; "utterly destroys" is the verb; and "the tall and verdant trees of the forest" is the object." The Sanskrit Language, the most philosophic of human tongues, or, as the Brāhmans not unreasonably say, "the language of the Gods," would easily and elegantly express the above sentence in three words. "The scorching fire of the thunder-cloud" might be thrown into one compound in the nominative case; the verb "utterly consumes" would be expressed by a preposition in composition with the verb *to consume;* and "the tall and verdant trees of the forest" might be formed into one compound in the accusative plural.

b. Although every simple sentence is reducible to three distinct parts, yet it is not easy to find a general term that will accurately apply to any of these parts except the verb. When the sentence is expressed by the verb "to be," the three parts may be called the *nominative*, the *verb*, and *attribute;* as, "James is diligent." When the sentence is expressed by any other neuter *verb*, the parts may be called *nominative*, *verb*, and *complement;* as, "James went from England to India." Lastly, when the sentence has an active verb, the parts are *agent*, *verb*, and *object;* as, "James purchased a horse." Perhaps the terms least liable to objection will be *nominative*, *verb*, and *complement;* yet even these would be found inadmissible when applied to the Hindūstānī, the Marhatti, and several other dialects of that class. In Persian, however, the latter terms are not inapplicable: we shall therefore employ them in this sense in the next paragraph, when treating of the arrangement of words.

c. A compound sentence, or period, consists of two or more simple sentences connected by a conjunction, expressed or understood; as, "Knowledge fills the mind with entertaining views, and administers to it a perpetual series of gratifications: it gives ease to solitude; fills a public station with suitable abilities; and, when it is mixed with complacency, it adds lustre to such as are possessed of it." It will be a useful exercise for the Student to analyze, by himself, the above compound sentence; which consists of five simple sentences, in all of which, *knowledge,* or its substitute *it,* is the nominative. The last two clauses make but one simple sentence, for they amount merely to this: "Knowledge, mixed with complacency, adds lustre to such as are possessed of it."

d. It may happen that the nominative to the verb is a short sentence; as, "What he says is of no consequence." So the complement may also be a sentence; as, "I know not what he thinks." These sentences are equivalent to, "His speech, or speaking, is of no consequence"; and, "I know not his thoughts." It may also happen that the nominative, or the complement, or both, may be qualified with a relative sentence, which is equivalent to an adjective. When such relative sentences or clauses occur they must not be confounded with a compound sentence. Thus, "God, who is Eternal and Invisible, created the world, which is perishable and visible," may at first sight appear a compound sentence; which is not the case, for it is equivalent to, "The Eternal and Invisible God created the perishable and visible world."

ARRANGEMENT OF WORDS.

49. As a preliminary step to our remarks on Persian Syntax, we may briefly notice the manner in which the words of that language are usually arranged in the formation of a sentence. In prose compositions the following rule generally holds; viz. In a simple sentence, the nominative is put first; then the object, or complement; and, lastly, the verb. Thus, in the sentence, "The Moghul purchased the parrot," the collocation of the words in Persian will be "The Moghul—the parrot—purchased," or مُغل طوطيرا خرِيد. Here *the Moghul* is the nominative, beginning the sentence;

طوطي را, *the parrot*, is the complement, or object, in the accusative case, governed by the verb خريد *purchased*, which comes last. So in the sentence, "Taimūr came to India," تيمور به هندوستان آمد; *Taimūr* is the nominative, *came* (آمد) is the verb, which is placed at the end of the sentence, and *to India* is its complement. It may happen that the subject, or the object of the sentence, or both, may be restricted by, or in combination with, various circumstances of time, place, motive, &c.; and the verb qualified by an adverb: still the above arrangement holds good; the nominative, with all its restricting circumstances, coming first; then the complement; and, lastly, the verb, with its qualifying word immediately before it. Words and phrases denoting time, manner, &c., when they apply to the whole sentence, and not to any particular part of it, are placed first; as, روزي در شهري درويشي بر دوكانِ بقّالي رفت "One day, in a certain city, a darwesh went to the shop of a certain trader." When the complement of a verb is a complete sentence it is put last, as in English; thus, آن مرد گفت مرا احمق مي پنداري "That man said, 'Do you consider me a fool?'" So in the sentence, پادشاهي درخواب ديد كه تمامِ دندانهاي او افتاده اند "A certain king saw in a dream that the whole of his teeth had dropped out," where the phrase "the whole of his teeth had dropped out" is the complement to the verb "saw," or "saw in a dream." When the object is qualified by a relative sentence, the object is placed before the verb, and the qualifying phrase after, as in the beginning of the Gulistan: پادشاهي را شنيدم كه بكشتنِ اسيري اشارت كرد "I have heard of a king who issued the order (made the signal) for the executing of a certain captive." In like manner, in يكي را از ملوكِ عجم حكايت كنند كه دستِ تطاول بمالِ رعيّت دراز كرد "They relate of one of the kings of Persia that he extended the hand of usurpation over the property of the people"; the relative phrase comes last.

a. In further illustration of the preceding general rule, together with its occasional exceptions, let us analyze the simple story of the

Villager and his Ass, page 22; and to make the matter less difficult, we shall still employ the Roman character. First sentence: *Dihkāne khare dāsht*—"A villager had an ass." This sentence is exactly like the first quoted above, only *the object* (*khare*) has not the sign *rā* attached to it, which, as we shall see hereafter, is not always necessary to distinguish the accusative case. Second sentence: *Az sababi bekharjī, khar rā barā-e charīdan babāghe sar mīdād*—"For the sake of economy (non-expenditure), (he) gave its head (*i.e.* its liberty) to the ass, for the purpose of grazing in a certain garden." In this sentence the subject, the verb, and the object are complex, or accompanied by circumstances. The nominative is, "the villager (qualified by the phrase), from motives of economy"; the verb is, *mīdād* "gave, *or* used to give," qualified by the word *sar* "head"; and the object, or complement, is, "to the ass, for the purpose of grazing in a certain garden." Third sentence: *Mardumāni bāgh khar rā mīzadand; wa az zarā'at ba dar mīkardand*—"The people of the garden used to beat the ass; and (they) used to send him forth from the cultivated ground." This is a compound sentence, consisting of two distinct assertions, connected by the conjunction *wa* "and." The nominative of both sentences is, "The people of the garden"; the object is, "the ass"; and in the last sentence, the verb *mīkardand* is qualified by the words, "out from the cultivated ground." Fourth sentence: *Roze dihkān posti sher rā bar khar bast; wa guft, Wakti shab barā-e charīdan tū bar ā-ī, wa, āwāz makun*—"One day the villager fastened the skin of a lion upon the ass; and said, At the time of night, you go forth for the purpose of grazing, and do not make a noise." Here, again, we have a compound sentence made up of two propositions, as in the preceding. We may observe that the words "one day," being applicable to the whole sentence, and not to any particular member of it, are placed first of all. The nominative is, "the villager"; the verb, "fastened"; and, "a lion's skin upon the ass" is the complement. The term *posti sher* has the *rā* added here, apparently without any necessity; but it so stands in the manuscript from which the story is extracted. In the second part of this compound sentence, the nominative is still "the villager"; the verb is *guft* "said"; and the rest of the sentence is the complement to that verb. This, as we have stated, is an exception to the general rule; viz. when the complement to a verb is a complete sentence, simple or compound, such complement follows the verb. Fifth sentence: *Hamchunān har shab bā posti sher ān khar babāgh mīraft*—"Thus, every night, with the lion's skin, the ass used to go into the garden." This sentence requires little remark. The nominative is *ān khar* "that ass," accompanied with circumstances; viz. "in that manner, with the lion's skin." *Har shab*, "every night," qualifies the whole sentence. Sixth sentence: *Harkī ka shab mīdīd, yakīn mīdānist ki īn sher ast*—"Whoever saw (him) by night thought for certain that this is a lion." A compound sentence; the nominative of the first part of which is "whoever"; the verb is "saw," qualified by the words, "by night"; and "him" is the object. In the second part, the nominative "he" is understood; the verb is "thought," qualified by the adverb "for certain"; and the complement (following the verb, as in the fourth sentence) is, "that this is a lion." Seventh sentence: *Shabe bāghbān orā dīd, wa az tars bar bālā-e darahkte raft*—"One night the gardener saw him; and from fear he went upon the top of a tree." Here the word *shabe* "one night," qualifies the whole compound sentence, and comes first of all. In the second clause, *bāghbān* (understood) is the nominative, with the accompanying circumstance, *az tars*, "from fear." Eighth sentence: *Dar asnā-e ān, khare dīgar ki dar ān nazdīkī būd, āwāz kard; wa khari dihkān nīz ba āwāz dar āmad; wa bāng zadan misli kharān girift*—"In the midst of this (mean while), another ass, which was in that vicinity, made a noise; and the ass of the villager also into braying came; and began to raise a cry in the manner of asses." This is a compound sentence, consisting of three simple sentences; in the first of which is placed *Dar asnā-e ān*, which qualifies the whole sentence. *Khare dīgar ki dar ān nazdīkī būd* is the nominative of the first sentence, qualified by a relative clause, which the Sanskrit would have expressed by a compound adjective. Ninth sentence: *Bāghbān orā shinākht, wā dānist ki īn kīst*—"The gardener recognised him, and knew who this was." A compound sentence: the complement to the verb *danist*, in the last clause, is *ki īn kīst*, which is placed after the verb. Tenth sentence: *Az darakht farod āmad, wa ān khar rā bisyār lat ba-zad*—"From the tree he came down, and very much did beat that ass with a stick." Eleventh sentence: *Az īnjā khiradmandān gufta and ki "kharān rā khāmoshī bih"*—"On this subject the wise have said, 'That for the asses silence is best.'" It is needless to add any remark on the last two sentences, which present no peculiarity that we have not already noticed.

50. We here subjoin the preceding story in the native character, which will afford the Student an easy example for his first lesson in translating. He ought, at the same time, to ascertain the exact meaning of each word, from the Vocabulary, and be able to parse the whole of them, by a reference to the preceding portion of the Grammar. In like manner let him analyze and translate Stories I. and II. (pp. 20 and 21); after which he may proceed to the Selections at the end of the work. When he has read, and carefully analyzed, from fifteen to twenty pages of the Selections, he may then with advantage peruse the rules of Syntax which follow this page, but *not till then*: for we hold it to be downright absurdity to make a person read the Syntax of a language before he knows a little of the language itself.

حِكايتِ دِهْقان و خر

(۱) دِهْقاني خري داشْت * (۲) از سببِ بي خَرْجِي
خررا براي چرِيدن به باغي سرِمي داد * (۳) مَرْدُمانِ
باغ خررا مِي زدنْد و از زراعت به در مِي كرْدنْد *

(۴) روزي دِهْقان پوسْتِ شيررا برخر بسْت و گُفْت وقْتِ شب براي چرِيدن تُو برآءى و آوازمكُن * (۵) هَمْچُنان هر شب باپوسْتِ شير آن خر به باغ مي رفْت * (٦) هركِه به شب مِي دِيد يقِين مِي دانِسْت كه اِين شير اسْت * (۷) شبي باغْبان اورا دِيد و از تَرْس بر بالائي درخْتي رفْت * (۸) در اثْنائي آن خري دِيگر كِه در آن نزْدِيكِي بُود آواز كرْد و خرِ دِهْقان نِيز به آواز در آمد و بانْگ زدن مِثْلِ خران گِرِفْت * (۹) باغْبان اورا شِناخْت و دانِسْت كِه اِين كِيسْت * (۱۰) از درخْت فرود آمد و آن خررا بِسْيار لت به زد * (۱۱) از اِينْجا خِرَدْمنْدان گُفْتَه انْد كه خران را خاموشِي بِه *

We may here observe, that the preposition به *ba*, "to," "at," "in," "by," which, in the preceding story, we have written separate, is frequently joined to its substantive; and the same may be said of the prefix مِي of the verb; as also of the negative particle نه *na*, "not," which, it seems optional to write separately or unite with the verb. When به and نه are joined to the following word, the weak ه is suppressed; thus, we may write به شب or بشب "by night." Lastly, the termination را *ra*, the sign of the Dative and Accusative, may be joined to the last letter of a word, or written separately; thus, باغْبانْرا or باغْبان را *bāghbān-rā*, "to the gardener."

CONSTRUCTION OF SUBSTANTIVES, ADJECTIVES, AND PREPOSITIONS.

51. As the adjectives in Persian are all indeclinable, the learner is freed from all anxiety on the score of Concord: he has merely to remember, that, as a general rule, adjectives follow the noun which they qualify, and the noun takes the mark of the *izāfat*, as explained in pages 27 and 31; thus, وزيرِ ناصح "the sincere minister"; رويِ خوب "a beautiful face"; طرّهٔ مشكبوي "a ringlet with the fragrance of musk."

a. In poetry it is not uncommon to place the adjective first, exactly as in English; thus, Firdausī has هشيوار دستور بر دست شاه "an intelligent counsellor by the hand of the king"; so, دانشمند پادشاه "a wise king." When the adjective thus precedes the substantive (which sort of construction is, in Persian, called "the inverted epithet"), the mark of the *izāfat* is not used.

b. We have already explained (pp. 50 and 51) the nature of compound adjectives: we may further observe here, that any noun with a particle prefixed to it may become an expressive epithet; as, مردِ بامال "a man possessed of wealth." Many epithets consist of three or more words; as, ملكِ بجنگ گرفته "a country taken in war"; so بندهٔ حلقه بگوش "a slave with a ring in his ear." So in the Bastán of Sa'dī we have حكيمِ سخن بر زبان آفرين "The Allwise, who endows the tongue with speech"; where the substantive حكيم has the rest of the line for its epithet. In fact, there is no limit to the extent to which the composition of epithets may be carried in this language; and it is necessary that, in every instance, the Student should be able to distinguish them, that he may add the mark of the *izāfat* to the preceding noun, which they serve to qualify.

L

c. Numeral adjectives precede the nouns to which they belong; and what is altogether at variance with our notions of concord, the noun is generally put in the singular number; as, صد سال "a hundred years," instead of صد سالها; so, ده درویش "ten darweshes," instead of درویشان; in which expressions the numeral word prefixed is sufficient to indicate the plurality of the noun, without adding the usual termination. In fact, we have frequently heard in our own language, among the common people, such phrases as "five pound," "ten mile": and the expressions, "a hundred horse," "three hundred cannon," &c. are allowed to be good English.

d. Sometimes a phrase from the Arabic, constructed according to the grammatical rules of that language, may be introduced as an epithet to a Persian substantive; thus, درویشِ مُسْتجابُ ٱلدَّعْوات "a derwesh, whose prayers are answered"; so, مردِ صادقُ ٱلقول "a man sincere in speech"; کریمُ ٱلنّفس "generous of soul."

e. The adjective pronouns این and آن precede their substantives; and there are a few adjectives of a pronominal nature which may optionally precede or follow; as, همه "all"; دیگر "other"; چند "some *or* several": thus, همه مردمان or مردمانِ همه "all the people"; so, زنِ دیگر or دیگر زن "the other woman"; روزِ چند or چند روز "some *or* several days."

52. Our word *than*, after the comparative degree, is expressed in Persian by از; thus, روشنتر از رخِ روز "more splendid than the cheek of day"; so, اي ملِك ما درین دُنیا بجیش از تُو کمتریم و بعَیش از تُو خوشتر "O king, we are, in this world, less than you as to pomp, but more happy in our enjoyments." The adjective به "good," is often used in the positive form when denoting comparison, as in the following maxim from the گلستان of Sa'dī: دروغِ مصلحت‌آمیز به از راستِ فتنه‌انگیز "Falsehood, fraught with good advice, is preferable to the truth,

when tending to excite strife"; so in the following sentence, خاموشي بِه از سخن بد است و سخنِ نيك بِه از خاموشي "Silence is better than evil speaking, and speaking well is better than silence."

a. The superlative degree, when used, governs the genitive, as in our own language; thus, نيكترينِ مردمان "the best of men"; so, گويند كه كمترينِ جانوران خراست "They say that the meanest of animals is the ass." The same rule applies to superlative forms from the Arabic; as, اشرفِ انبيا "the most illustrious of the prophets."

b. Sometimes the superlative is employed merely in an intensive sense, like a simple adjective; in which case the *izāfat* is not used, as in the couplet—

نگويم گرامِيترين گوهري
سپردم بنامِيترين شوهري

"I will not say that I have given an exceedingly noble lady to a most highly-renowned husband."

53. In Persian, the particles called prepositions are, strictly speaking, very few in number, probably not more than those already given in page 51, No. 42: viz. از "from"; با "with"; بر "on"; به "in," "into"; بي "without"; تا "till," "as far as"; جز "except," "besides"; and در "in"; which invariably take the simple or nominative form of a noun or pronoun after them; as, از بغداد تا شيراز "from Baghdād to Shīrāz"; با تو خواهم رفت "I will go with thee." Such other words as are used like prepositions are really nouns, and in construction require the *izāfat*; as, نزدِ وزير "near the minister," which is an elliptical form of expression for به نزدِ وزير "in the vicinity of the minister"; so زيرِ زمين "under the earth"; بالاي سرش "above his head"; پيشِ من "before me," that is, در پيشِ من "in front of me." The Student will do well in committing to memory the simple prepositions, and

in recollecting that the rest require the *izāfat* when they govern a noun.

a. It may be proper to observe that the particle جُز is a species of noun, denoting "other," "else," and consequently we should expect it to be followed by the *izāfat;* which, however, is not the case; thus, in the following line from Sa'dī—

حَيف باشد كه جُز نِكو گويد

"Pity it were he should speak other than (what is) good"—
we know, from the metre, that جُز has no *izāfat.* We may farther mention, that the particle تا is more generally used as a conjunction, with various significations, which it is beyond our province here to detail.

PRONOUNS.

54. We shall now treat more particularly of those classes of pronouns, the explanation of which we passed over in Nos. 32 and 34; the others having nothing peculiar in their construction. The following may be denominated *affixed,* because, with the exception of the 3d plural, they are always joined to some word or other in the sentence in which they are employed.

	SINGULAR.	PLURAL.
1.	ـَم "my *or* me."	مان "our *or* us."
2.	ـَت "thy *or* thee."	تان "your *or* you."
3.	ـَش "his, her, its," *or* "him, her, it."	شان "their *or* them."

When these pronominal terminations are joined to nouns they generally correspond with our possessives, *my, thy,* &c.; as, دِلَم "my heart"; كتابَت "thy book"; سرَش "his, her, *or* its head": the plural terminations are very rarely used, their place being supplied by the nom. pl. of the personal pronouns employed as nouns; thus, دِلهاي ما "our hearts *or* hearts of us"; اسْپانِ شُما

"your horses *or* horses of you"; حالِ ایشان "the condition of them." When the noun ends in ه imperceptible, the terminations م, ت, ش, become ام, ات, and اش; as, جامه ام "my robe," &c.: and if the noun ends in ا or و long, they become یم, یت, یش; as, پایم "my foot"; مُویت "thy hair"; رویش "his *or* her face." These are euphonic principles, similar in their nature to those already detailed in p. 47. *b.* with respect to the verbal terminations added to substantives, adjectives, and participles.

55. When the terminations ـَم, ـَت, ـَش, are joined to the persons of a verb, they generally correspond with the dative or accusative case of the personal pronouns; as, دیدمت "I saw thee"; گُفتمش "I said to him." It appears, then, that these affixes may be employed to denote either the possessives *my, thy, his*, &c., or the dative and accusative, *me, thee*, &c., according to circumstances. When employed in the latter sense, they may be joined not only to the verb which governs them, but to any word in the sentence, with the exception of the simple prepositions, already noticed, and a few of the conjunctions, as وَ "and," یا "or," &c.; thus, دربانم رها نکرد "the porter did not admit me," or, verbatim, "the porter to me guidance not made"; so خاکش چُنان بخُورد "the earth has so much consumed it." In instances of this kind the Student must be guided by the context; as, دربانم, in the first of the above examples, may also mean "my porter": but when Sa'dī (from whom the expression is taken) states, in the sentence immediately preceding, "that he went to wait on the *great man*," the true meaning of the expression will be obvious.

56. The invariable word خُود, in Persian, corresponds with our reciprocal pronoun *self;* as, مَن خُود "I myself"; تُو خُود "thou thyself," &c. It may also be the nominative to any person of the verb, the verbal termination sufficiently shewing the sense; as,

خُود رفتم "I myself went"; خُود رفتند "they themselves went." The usage of the Persian language requires the employment of خود, on certain occasions, as a substitute for a possessive pronoun; thus, زرگر به خانهٔ خود رفت "the goldsmith went to his own house," literally, "to the house of self"; من از باغِ خُود مي آمدم "I was coming from my garden *or* from garden of self."

a. The following is a general rule for the employment of خُود. If, in a simple sentence, a personal pronoun in an oblique case (as, *me*, *thee*, *of me*, or *my*, &c.) be required, and if it be of the same person with the nominative of the sentence, the place of such pronoun must be supplied in Persian by خُود; thus, "I am writing my letter," من خطِّ خُود مي نويسم, *i.e.* "I write the letter of (my) self"; so زَيد غُلامِ خُودرا زد "Zaid beat his (own) slave"; مرْدُمان بخانهٔ خُود رفتند "the people went to their own houses."

b. It is almost unnecessary to state, that when the two pronouns are not of the same person, or rather when the latter pronoun does not belong to the nominative of the sentence, خُود cannot be used; as, "Zaid beat your slave," زَيد غُلامِ شُمارا زد; so, "Zaid beat his (meaning another person's) slave," زَيد غُلامِ اورا زد. We may observe, that instead of خُود, the words خويش, خويشتن, and خُوي are sometimes used: خُودش also occurs, but only in the 3d pers. sing.; as, زيدرا در خانهٔ خودش ديدم "I saw Zaid in his own house"; literally, "I saw Zaid in the house of his self." This sentence, by the way, would at first sight seem to be at variance with part of the preceding rule; but the expression amounts to this, "I saw that Zaid was in his own house," *or* "I saw Zaid, who was in his own house."

c. We find in the last London edition of the Gulistan, Book III. Ap. 8, the following suspicious reading: يكي از حُكما پسرش را نهي كرد

"One of the sages made a prohibition to his son," where the use of the pronoun کش is wrong. We have consulted nine manuscripts of the original in our possession, not one of which has the pronoun کش. In M. Semelet's edition of the Gulistan, printed at Paris, 1828, the same error is repeated, although the work pretends to great critical accuracy.

57. With regard to the demonstrative pronouns اِین and آن, we have little further to add. (Vide No. 33.) When the name of an irrational being, or of an inanimate object, has been mentioned, and reference is made to it afterwards by a pronoun, as *he, she, it, they*, &c., اِین and آن, with their plurals, are generally used, seldom او or ایشان; thus, شیر گُفت مُصَوِّرِ اِین اِنسانسْت "The lion said, The painter of it (alluding to a picture) is (was) a man"; so حُکما از تاویلِ آن عاجِز ماندند "The wise men were at a loss in the explaining of it."

a. The phrases از آنِ تُو ,از آنِ من or ,آنِ تو ,آنِ من, &c., are equivalent to our words *mine, thine*, &c.; as, مسْندِ مِصر آنِ تُوست "The throne of Egypt is thine"; so in Story 71 of the Selections we have the phrases, اِین خانه اوّل از آنِ که بُود "Whose house was this originally?" گُفت از آنِ جدّم "He said, That of my grand-father's." چونِ او بگُذشْت از آنِ که شُد "When he died, whose did it become?" گُفت از آنِ پدرم "He said, That of my father's," &c.

58. The words که and چه, in Persian, generally correspond, in the nominative case, with our relative pronouns *who* and *which*; but Dr. Lumsden shews that they are merely *connectives*, and have the personal pronouns understood after them; thus, Sa'dī has ملِك زاده را دِیدم که عقل داشْت "I saw a prince who possessed wisdom": after کِه the personal pronoun او is understood; as,

كه او عقل داشت "that he possessed wisdom." As the personal pronoun, however, is generally left out, the particles كه and چه have been considered, by some oriental grammarians, as *relatives*. The following sentence from the Gulistan, to which many others might be added, confirms Dr. Lumsden's views on this subject: ابلهي كو روزِ روشن شمع كافوري نهد "The fool who burns (sets up) a camphor candle in a clear day"; where كو is a contraction of كه او; literally, "The fool, that he burns," &c., where the mere كه, if it were a relative, would have equally answered the metre.

a. When the Persians have occasion to express a sentence, containing what, in European Grammars, is called a relative pronoun in an oblique case, they employ the particle كه, together with the corresponding personal pronoun, as may be seen in the following examples from the Gulistan:—1st, In the Genitive Case: بس ناموركه زيرِ زمين دفن كرده اند كزهستيش بروي زمينِ يك نشان نماند "Many a renowned personage have they deposited beneath the dust, of whose existence (literally, that of his existence) no trace (now) remains on the face of the earth." Again, Sa'dī says— آن نه من باشم كه روزِ جنگ بيني پشتِ من "I am not he whose back you will see in the day of battle;" *or*, literally, "that you should see my back." 2dly, In the Dative: اي كه شخصِ منت حقير نمود "O (thou) to whom my person appeared worthless!" literally, "that my person appeared to thee." 3dly, In the Accusative: آن كه چون پسته ديدمش همه مغز "He whom I beheld all fat, like the pistachio nut;" literally, "He that I saw him." 4thly, In the Ablative: آنكه در وي مظنهء خطر است "That (proceeding) in which there is an idea of danger."

b. The compound terms هركه and هرچه, when unaccompanied by a substantive, correspond to our words *whosoever* and *whatsoever*; the former generally denoting rational beings, and the latter inferior animals, or lifeless matter; thus,

هرکه دست از جان بشوید هرچه در دل دارد بگوید "Whoever shall wash his hands of life, the same will utter whatever he has on his mind." If we could trust the genuineness of the following sentence from Sa'dī, it would appear that هرچه may sometimes be applied to persons as well as things; thus, in the Second Book of the Gulistan (Ap. 37), an experienced old Doctor recommends to his pupil the following ingenious method of getting rid of his friends:

هرچه درویشانند ایشانرا وامي بده وآنچه توانگرانند از ایشان چیزي بخواه

"Whosoever are poor, to them give a small loan; and of those who are rich ask something": but MSS. by no means agree in this reading; and our finest MS. has it thus,

درویشانرا وامي بده واز توانگران چیزي بخواه

"To the poor lend a little, and of the rich ask something."

c. When the substantive is expressed after هر, the particle که may follow, whether the substantive be animate or inanimate; as, هرچیزکه "every thing which." When the termination ي *majhūl* (p. 30. *a.*) is added to a noun, and که or چه follows, the substantive is thereby rendered more definite or specific; as, حسد رنجیست که از مشقت آن جز بمرگ نتوان رست "Envy is such a (peculiar) torment, that it is impossible to escape from its pangs, except by death." We may observe in conclusion, on the subject of the relative, or rather *the want of a relative*, in Persian, that if که and چه are to be considered as mere connective particles (a matter on which our researches do not warrant us to give a decisive opinion), it need not be wondered at that the rules respecting their agreement with their antecedents should be liable to many deviations.

59. We have already stated (No. 34) that که and چه are used as interrogatives; the former applicable to persons, and the latter to irrational beings: but if the noun be expressed, چه may be used in both instances; as, چه‌مرد "What man?" The word کدام

is also used as an interrogative: it is applicable to every gender and number; as, کُدام مَرْد "What *or* Which man?" کُدام کار "What *or* Which business?" کِه and چِه, when used interrogatively, are to be considered as substantives singular or plural, according to the nouns which they represent; as, آن اَسْپِ کِه باشد "Whose horse is that?" کِرا مِي گويند "To whom are they speaking?" ايشان کِيند "Who are they?" از بهرِ چه آمده "On account of what are you come?" چرا رفتي "For what did you go?" The interrogative particle آيا corresponds with the Latin *an, num,* &c.; as, آيا بادشاه آمده است *An rex venit?* "Is the King arrived?"

CONCORD OF VERBS.

60. If the nominative to a verb, in Persian, be expressive of rational beings, or of living creatures in general, the verb agrees with it in number and person, as in our own language; also, two or more nouns in the singular, denoting animals, require the verb to be put in the plural number; as, برادران برنجيدند "The brothers were vexed"; جانورانِ جنگل آواز نمودند "The animals of the forest made a noise"; زرگر ونجّار بُتانرا گرفتند "The goldsmith and the carpenter seized the images."

61. When two or more inanimate nouns have a common verb, the latter is generally put in the singular, as in the following lines from Sa'dī:

گرچه سيم و زر زِسنگ آيد همي در همه سنگي نباشد زر و سيم

"Although silver and gold be produced from stone, yet every stone will not yield gold and silver."

تامرد سُخن نگفته باشد عيب وهنرش نهفته باشد

"Until a man hath spoken, his defects and his skill are concealed."

62. We have already mentioned, that when a numeral adjective

precedes a noun, the latter does not require the plural termination: but if the noun denote rational beings, and be the subject of a verb, the verb is put in the plural; as, ده درویش در گلیمي بخسپند "Ten darweshes will sleep on one blanket." Irrational animals, and especially inanimate things, generally take the verb in the singular; as, صد هزار اسب حاضر شد "A hundred thousand horses were ready"; so, دو هزار غرفه وهزار ایوان بود "There were two thousand rooms and a thousand vestibules."

a. Arabic plurals, introduced into Persian, follow a similar rule; that is, if they denote animals, and more particularly rational beings, the verb is put in the plural: but inanimate nouns generally take the singular; as, حکما گفته اند "The wise men have said"; از آمدن بهار از رفتن دي اوراق حیات ما میگردد طي "By the approach of spring, and the passing by of December, the leaves of our life come to a close."

b. The classical scholar will observe that there is a resemblance between the concord of a Persian verb with its nominative, and that of the Greek; the plurals of the neuter gender, in the latter language, requiring the verb to be in the singular. The Persian has another peculiarity, not unlike the German; viz. when inferiors speak *to* or *of* their superiors, the verb is employed in the plural, generally in the third person. Thus a servant, in speaking of his master, would say, صاحب خانه بیرون رفته اند "The master of the house is (are) gone out." So, in Story 26, we have a similar construction, viz. جهان پناه بسیار خوار هستند که نه تخم گذاشتند نه خرما "Your Majesty is a great glutton, having left neither dates nor stones"; literally, "The Asylum of the universe *are* a great glutton," &c. This style, however, does not seem to have belonged to the classic period of the language.

GOVERNMENT OF VERBS.

63. The only peculiarity in the government of verbs, in Persian, is, that a transitive or active verb does not always require, as in Greek and Latin, that its complement should have the termination of the accusative case; thus, ساقِيا ساغرِ شرابِ بيار "O cup-bearer, bring a goblet of wine;" where ساغرِ شراب has not the sign of the accusative case affixed. So in the following lines from Sa'dī:

عُذرِ تقْصيرِ خِدْمت آوَرْدم كِه ندارم بطاعت اِسْتِظهار

عاصيان از گُناه تَوبه كُنند عارِفان از عِبادت اِسْتِغفار

"I have brought (only) an excuse for the defect of my service; for in my obedience I have no claim: the wicked express contrition for their sins; the holy beg forgiveness on the score of their (imperfect) devotions." In this extract the four words, *excuse, claim contrition,* and *forgiveness,* have not the sign of the accusative case added to any of them in the original. Again, in the following sentences the accusative case is accompanied by its appropriate sign: غُلامرا بدَرْيا انْداخْتنْد "They threw the slave into the sea"; دَرْويش سنْگرا با خُود نِگاه مي‌داشْت "The darwesh preserved the stone in his possession." Lastly, in the following extract from the Story, p. 71, we have the same word used in different places, first without, and then with the را; thus,

دِهْقاني خري داشْت * مرْدُمانِ باغ خررا مِيزدنْد "A certain villager had an ass. The people of the garden used to beat the ass." In the first sentence we have خري داشْت, without the را; and in the second we have خررا مِيزدنْد, where the را is added. Hence we see that sometimes the object takes the termination را, and sometimes not; and the following appear to us to be the general principles that regulate the insertion or omission of that termination:

a. When we wish to render the object definite, emphatic, or particular, را is added; for instance, شراب بيار signifies, "Bring wine"; but شرابرا بيار means, "Bring *the* wine." So in the Story, دهقاني خري داشت "A villager had an ass," the را is not needed; but in the next sentence, مردمانِ باغ خررا ميزدند "The people of the garden were beating *the* ass," the را is used, because the object is now more definite.

b. It is a general rule to add را to the object of an active verb, whenever any ambiguity would arise from its omission; or, in other words, when the action described by the verb is such as might be performed by either the agent or object; thus, زرگر نجاررا بزد "The goldsmith struck the carpenter"; مرد شيررا كشت "The man slew the lion"; اسكندر دارارا بيفكند "Iskandar overthrew Dárá," or, as the Latin Grammar hath it, *Alexander Darium vicit.* In these examples, if we omit the را we are left merely to infer the sense from the arrangement, which, in ordinary prose, might form a sufficient criterion, but not in verse.

c. When the object of an active verb is a personal pronoun, or its substitute خود, the termination را is always used; as, مرا نمي شناسي "Dost thou not know me?" ترا ديدم "I saw thee"; اورا گرفتند "They seized him"; نگاهدار مارا ز راه خطا "Preserve us from the path of error"; فلان شخص خودرا كشته است "Such a person has killed himself."

d. Having stated what we consider the general principles which regulate the insertion of را as the sign of the accusative case, the rule for its non-insertion may be inferred; viz. the insertion of را is not necessary whenever the nature of the sentence is such as to enable the reader or hearer to comprehend the sense clearly without it, except when we wish to particularize or limit the object, or when it is a personal pronoun. Lastly, in such compound verbs as we mentioned in p. 64. *o*, like حُکم کَرْدن, &c., the را is never added to the substantive.

64. The termination را is added to a substantive to denote the dative case as well as the accusative. On such occasions its insertion is indispensably necessary; as, ظالِمي را حِكايت کُنند "They relate a story with regard to a certain oppressor"; so in this phrase, هزار روپِيه را اَسْپي خرِيدم "For a thousand rupees I bought a horse."

a. When a verb governs an accusative, and at the same time a dative case, the termination را is seldom, if ever, added to both cases; thus, if the accusative be indefinite, or does not necessarily require را, according to the principles already laid down, then the dative has the را added; as, آن مرْدرا كِتابي دادم "I gave a book to that man." So, هرِيك ضَعِيفهرا يك نِيمه دِهند "Let them give a half to each woman." If the accusative necessarily require را, the dative must be formed by a preposition, as به "to"; thus, لَعْل را به آن زن دِهند "Let them give the ruby to that woman"; so, كِتاب را بمن بِدِه "Give me the book." In these last examples, the words كِتاب and لعل being definite, require the addition of را; and the dative cases are formed by prefixing the particle به *ba* to the pronouns من and آن.

65. When the object is in a state of construction with another noun, or with an adjective, and from its nature requires را, that termination is added to the latter noun or adjective; as follows; زَيد پِسرِ وزِير را دِيدم "I saw Zaid, the son of the minister"; so, درجنّت نخواهِي يافْت گُلْگشْتِ مُصلّارا "In Paradise you will

not find the rosy bowers of Musallā." In this rule there is much sound philosophy; for when one substantive governs another in the genitive, the two are to be considered as one modified noun; thus, in the following sentence, from the 1st Book of the Gulistan, يكي از مُلُوكِ خُراسان سُلْطان مَحْمُودِ سبكتكين را بخواب دِيد "One of the kings of Khurāsān saw in a dream Sultān Mahmūd (the son) of Sabaktagīn," the three words سُلْطان مَحْمُودِ سبكتكين are viewed as one modified noun, and the termination را is very properly placed at the end. In like manner, a substantive, accompanied by an adjective, is to be considered as a single specified noun; and, in construction, the termination را, when requisite, is placed at the end; thus, قاضي زنِ همسايه‌را طلب كرْد "The Judge summoned the neighbouring woman." So, however complex the adjective may be, the را is placed at the end; thus, from Sa'dī, تني چند از مردانِ واقِعه دِيده و جنگ آزموده‌را بفرستادند "They sent forward several individuals from among men who had seen service and had experienced war": here the complement or object of the verb, بفرستادند, consists of the whole preceding sentence; and the را is affixed last of all, the more to define that complex object, now viewed as a single whole.

66. It remains for us to notice a few verbal expressions which some Grammarians consider as tenses, and which we omitted in the paradigm, as of small importance. In Dr. Lumsden's Grammar, Vol. I. p. 93, &c., we have two tenses of a potential mood, present and past, formed respectively by adding the contracted infinitive to the aorist and preterite of the verb; تَوَانستن (root تَوان) "to be able"; as, تَوَانم رفت "I am able to go," *or* "I can go"; تَوَانستم رفت "I was able to go," *or* "I could go." But, in truth, we are more inclined to consider these as sentences than tenses. In a large and closely written Persian manuscript, which treats of the grammar of that language, called the *Miftāh-ut-tarkīb*, compiled,

as the writer tells us, by *Shewā Rām*, poetically named *Jauhar*, there is a tense called the Continuative Imperative, or Imperative of duration, formed by prefixing the particle مِي to the future perfect; thus, from رفته باشد "He shall have gone," comes مِي رفته باشد "Let him continue going." This tense is also called, according to Jauhar, *Istimrārī-e-Maznūn* (اِسْتِمرارِي مظنُون), which is a sort of imperfect or continuative potential; as, "He may be going"; the meaning of it in Hindustānī being given, جاتا هوئي وُه. The ordinary imperative may denote continuity by prefixing مِي ;
شبها بردرگاه الهي دادِ گدائي مِي دِه و روزها در بارگاه خُود بداد گدایان مِي رس
"Nightly at the threshold of God continue giving forth the gift of thy unworthiness; and daily in thine own court constantly attend to (the administration of) justice among the poor."

67. When the verbs خواستن "to intend *or* wish," تَوَانستن "to be able," بایستن and شایستن "to be proper *or* fit," are followed by an infinitive, the final ـَن of the infinitive is rejected; as, خواهم رفت "I will go," *or* "I intend to go"; تَوَانم نَوِشت "I can write." The verbs بایستن and تَوَانستن are generally used impersonally, in the third person singular of the aorist or present; as, بايد كَرْد "One ought to do." The mere root, تَوَان, of تَوَانستن is also used impersonally; as, تَوَان كَرْد "One may do." We have reason to believe, from observing the usage of the best writers of the language, that when the infinitive precedes the above verbs, the final ـَن is not rejected; as, اِيـن كاركَرْدن نميتَوَانم "I cannot do this deed"; so, تُراجائي فِرِستادن نميخواهم "I do not intend to send you anywhere."

68. The infinitive, in Persian, is to be considered merely as a verbal noun, and construed like any other substantive. It

corresponds more with the verbal noun of the Latin, formed from the supine by changing the *um* into *io* or *us*, than it does with the infinitive, gerund, or supine of that language; as, in this sentence, بادشاهي به کُشتنِ اسيري اِشارت کرد "A certain king made the signal for the killing of a captive"; which, by Gentius, is rendered into Latin, *Captivum interficere signum dederat;* but the literal rendering is, *Ad captivi interfectionem*, or *De captivi interfectione;* hence the infinitive of an active verb, in Persian, governs a genitive, and not an accusative, as in most European tongues.

69. Conjunctions, in Persian, are applied as in English or Latin; that is, when any thing contingent, doubtful, &c. is denoted, the conjunction is usually followed by the subjunctive mood (aorist and past potential); as, به ناني بِساز تا نکُني پُشت به خدمت دوتا "Be satisfied with a loaf (of bread), that you may not bend your back in servitude"; so, اگر روزي بدانِش در فزودي زِنادان تنگ روزتر نبُودي "If the augmentation of wealth depended upon knowledge, none would be so distressed as the ignorant."

70. When a person has occasion to relate what he has heard from another, the usage of the Persian, like that of most oriental languages, requires that it should be done in the dramatic style. This will be easily understood from the following examples: "Zaid tells me that he will not come," زَيد مرا ميگويد که نخواهم آمد; literally, "Zaid says to me that 'I will not come.'" From the employing of the dramatic, instead of the narrative style, it will often happen that the Persian will differ widely from the English in the use of the persons and tenses of the verb, which may be seen from the few following examples; viz. "Zaid said that his brother was not in the house," زَيد گُفت که برادرِ من در خانه نيست; literally, "Zaid said, 'My brother is not in the house.'" So,

"A poet committed a crime (on which account) the king ordered the executioner to put him to death in his (the king's) presence," شاعِري تقصيري كرد پادشاه جلادرا فرمود كه رو بروي من اورا بكش; *i.e.* "The king ordered the executioner thus, 'Put him to death in my presence.'" It would be needless to add more examples of this kind: the learner has merely to recollect, as a general principle, that the person who relates a conversation that has occurred commonly gives the *ipsa verba* of the parties of whom he is speaking.

P. S. When the Student has read this Work through, as directed in the last page of the Preface, he will know enough of Persian to understand the numerous idioms and phrases, from that language, introduced into Hindūstānī. Should he, however, be induced to persevere in his Persian studies, let him proceed to the *Gulistān* of Sa'dī, and, after that, to the *Anwāri Suhailī* of Husain Wā'iz. In poetry, perhaps the best book to begin with is the *Bostān* of Sa'dī; then the *Iskandar-nāma* of Nizāmī, or Firdausi's *Shāhnāma;* to conclude with the *Dīwān* of Hafiz. I mention these, not merely because they are standard works, but, being in print, they are more likely to be met with than manuscripts.

D. F.

حِکایاتِ لطیف در عِبارتِ سلیس

۱ پِسرِ شخصي در چاه اُفتاد * آن شخص گُفت ــ اَي فرزندِ عَزیز ــ جائي نه رَوي ــ تا دلو و رَسَن بیارم *

۲ از مُعلّمي پُرسیدند که تُو بُزرگتري یابرادرِ تُو؟ گُفت من بُزُرگترم ــ امّا چُون یکسالِ دِیگر بر وَي بِگُذرد با من برابر خواهد شُد *

۳ زني بدرُوي و بدخُوي بِیمار شُد * بشَوهر گُفت اگر من بِمیِرم تُوهمِین چُون خواهِي زِیست؟ گُفت اگرنه میِري چُون خواهم زِیست؟

۴ روباه بچّهٔ ــ با مادرِ خُود گُفت مرا حِیلهٔ بِیاموز که چُون بکشاکشِ سگ درمانیم خودرا از و بِرهانیم ــ گُفت آن حِیلهٔ فراونست ــ امّا بِهترِینِ همه آنست که در خانهٔ خُود نِشیِني

۵ دَرویشي بِرهنه خواجهٔ را گُفت اگر من به درِ خانهٔ تُو بِمیِرم ــ مرا چه کُنِي؟ گُفت تُرا کفن کُنم ــ گُفت مرا در زِندِگي پیِراهني پوشان وچُون بِمیِرم بي کفنم در خاك سِپار ــ خواجه بخندید واورا پیِراهني داد *

۶ شخصي را پُرسیدند که چُون مردُم براي شُستنِ اندام در حَوض درآید ــ نظر در کُدام جانِب نُماید؟ گُفت اگر دانا بَوَد ــ به جانِبِ جامه و دستارِ خُود نظر دارد ــ گُفتند چرا؟ گُفت تا دُزدي نه برد *

B

۷ آورده اند که افلاطون وقتی زاهدی‌را دید که میگفت — خداوندا مرا از دوستانِ من نگاه دار * افلاطون گفت ای زاهد — این چه دعاست که میگوئی ؟ زاهد جواب داد احتراز از دشمنان ممکن است امّا از دوستان ممکن نیست *

۸ نوشیروان از بزرجمهر پرسید که شجاعت چیست * گفت قوّتِ دل * گفت چرا قوّتِ دست نمیگوئی * گفت اگر دل قوّی نیست قوّة در دست نمی ماند *

۹ مسخرهٔ با زنی شادی کرد * بعد از چهار ماه زنِ او پسر زائید * شوهررا گفت — این پسررا چه نام خواهی داشت * گفت پیک — چرا که راهِ نُه ماه در چهار ماه طی کرد *

۱۰ شخصی از افلاطون پرسید — که سالهای بسیار در جهاز بودی و سفرِ دریا کردی * در دریا چه عجائب دیدی * گفت عجب همین بود — که از دریا بکنارهٔ سلامت رسیدم *

۱۱ گویند شخصی بدرِ خانهٔ امیری چند بار رفت * دربانان گفتند در خواب است * ظریف گفت باو بگوئید — نو که این قدر از خواب محظوظی چرا نمی میری *

۱۲ گدائی بر دروازهٔ توانگری رفت و سؤال کرد * از اندرونِ خانه جواب آمد که بی‌بی در خانه نیست * گدا گفت پارهٔ نان سؤال کرده بودم بی‌بی‌را نخواستم که چنین جواب یافتم *

۱۳ زشت روی پیشِ طبیب رفت و گفت — بر زشت ترین جای مرا دُملی شده است — دوا بده * طبیب بر روی او نظر کرد

وگُفت — دُروغ میگوئی * روی تو می بینم برآن هیچ دُمّل نیست *

۱۴ شیری و مردی دریکخانه تصویرِ خودها دیدند * مرد شیررا گُفت می بینی شُجاعتِ انسان که شیررا تابع کرده است * شیر گُفت مُصوّرِ این انسان است * اگر شیر مُصوّر بودی اینچنین نبودی *

۱۵ طبیبی هرگاه بگورستان رفتی — چادر برسر و روی خود کردی * مردمان پُرسیدند که سببِ این چیست * گُفت از مُردگانِ این گورستان شرم میکنم — زیراکه از دوای من مُرده اند *

۱۶ احولی بُود که یک مُرغ پیشِ او درآمد * شخصی ازو پُرسید که چرا احول یک را دو می بیند * احول گُفت اگر این سُخن راست می بُود — پس این دُو مُرغ را چهار میدیدم *

۱۷ از حکیمی سُوال کردند که کُدام طعام طَیّب و لذیذ است * گُفت جُوع — یعنی هرگاه گُرسنگی غالب شود — هر طعام که خورند لذیذ و طَیّب باشد — و در ذائقه خُوش درآید *

۱۸ شخصی پیشِ قاضی آمد وگُفت — من گُرسنه ام چیزی بدِه که بخورم * قاضی گُفت ای ابله دیوانه شُده ؟ نشنیدهٔ که بخانهٔ قاضی سوای سوگند چیزی نمیخورند * محظوظ شُد ورفت *

۱۹ مشهور است که شخصی اِسکندر را گُفت — تو بادشاهی بُزرگ زنانِ بسیار را بعقد درآر — تا تُرا فرزندان شوند و از تُو یادگار مانند * گُفت — یادگارِ من عدل است و نیکنامی — زشت باشد کسی که برهمه مردمان غالب آمده باشد بآخر زبونِ زنان گردد *

۲۰ درویشی نزدِ بخیلی رفت و چیزی سُوال کرد * بخیل گُفت اگر

یك سُخن مرا قبول کُنی هرچِه بِگوئی خواهم کَرد * دَرویش پُرسید آن سُخن چیست * گُفت گاهی از من چیزی مخواه ـــ دِیگر هرچِه بِگوئی بِکُنم *

۲۱ روزی پادشاهی مع شاهزاده بشِکار رفت * چون هَوَا گرم شُد پادشاه و شاهزاده لبادهء خُودرا بر دوشِ مسخرهء نِهادند * پادشاه تبسّم کَرد و گُفت ـــ اَي مسخره ـــ بر تُو بارِ یك خر است * گُفت بلکِه بارِ دُو خر *

۲۲ کُوزیرا گُفتند میخواهی کِه پُشتِ تُو راست شَوَد یا پُشتِ دِیگر مَردُمان همچُو پُشتِ تُو کُوز گَردد * گُفت میخواهم کِه پُشتِ دِیگر مَردُمان کُوز گَردد ـــ تا از آن چشم کِه دِیگران مرا مِی بِینند ـــ من انهارا بِه بِینم *

۲۳ روزی پادشاهی از شاعِری رنجید * جلّادرا فرمود کِه رُو بروی من بِکُش * جلّاد براي شمشیر آوردن رفت * شاعِر حاضِرانرا گُفت ـــ تا شمشیر آورده شَوَد مرا سِیلهاي بِزنید کِه پادشاه خُوش شَوَد * پادشاه تبسّم نمُود و تقصِیرِ او بخشید *

۲۴ پادشاهی با وزِیر خُرما میخُورد و تُخمِ خُرما نزدِ وزِیر مِی انداخت * بعدِ خُوردن وزِیررا گُفت ـــ بِسیار خوار هستِي زِیرا کِه تُخمِ خُرما بِسیار پیشِ تُو اُفتاده اند * وزِیر گُفت نه ـــ جهان پناه بِسیار خوار هستند کِه نه تُخم گُذاشتند نه خُرما *

۲۵ شخصِي مرتبهء بُزُرگ یافت * دوستِي براي تهنِیَت پیشِ او رفت * آن شخص پُرسید کِیستِي ـــ و چِرا آمدهء ؟ دوستِ او شرمنده

گردید و گفت ـــ مرا نمي شناسي ـــ دوست قدیم تو ام ـــ براي تعزیت نزد تو آمده ام ـــ شنیده ام که کور شده *

٢٦ شخصي دستار درویشي گرفت و گریخت * درویش بگورستان رفت و نشست * مردمان اورا گفتند که آن شخص دستار ترا بطرف باغ برد ـــ در گورستان چرا نشسته و چه میکني * گفت او نیز آخر اینجا خواهد آمد ـــ ازین سبب اینجا نشسته ام *

٢٧ نقاشي در شهري رفت و آنجا پیشه طبابت آغاز کرد * بعد چند روز شخصي از وطن او در آن شهر رسید و اورا دید و پرسید که حالا چه پیشه میکني ؟ گفت طبابت * پرسید چرا ؟ گفت از براي آنکه اگر درین پیشه تقصیري میکنم ـــ خاك آنرا مي پوشد *

٢٨ سلطان سکندر ذو القرنین روزي بر دیوانه گذر کرد وگفت ـــ اي دیوانه از من چیزي بخواه * گفت مگسان تشویشم میدهند بگو که ندهند * سلطان گفت اي دیوانه چیزي طلب کن که در حکم ما باشد * دیوانه گفت هرگاه مگسي در اختیار تو نیست از تو چه خواهم *

٢٩ روزي شخصي با خود میگفت که هرچه در زمین و آسمان است همه براي من است ـــ مرا بسیار بزرگ خدا آفرید * در آن اثنا پشه بر بیني او نشست و گفت ـــ ترا چنین غرور نشاید ـــ زیرا که هرچه در زمین و آسمان است خدا براي تو آفرید ـــ بلکه ترا براي من * نداني که از تو بزرگترام *

٣٠ شاعري تونگري را مدح کرد هیچ نیافت * پس هجو کرد ـــ تونگر اورا هیچ نگفت * روز دیگر شاعر بر دروازه او رفت و نشست *

توَنگر گُفت اَي شاعِر — مدْح کرْدِي — هیچ تُرا ندادم — هجْو کرْدِي هیچ نگُفتم — حالاً چرا اِینْجا نِشستهٔ؟ گُفت حالاً مِیخواهم کِه اگر بمیرِي مرْثِیَهٔ تُو بِگویَم *

۳۱ نابِینائي در شبِ تار چراغ در دسْت و سبُو بر دوش گرِفته در بازار میرفت * شخْصي از وَي پُرسید کِه اَي احْمق روز و شب در چشْمِ تُو یکْسان اسْت * از چِراغ تُرا فائِده چِیست؟ نابِینا خنْدِید و گُفت — اِین چِراغ براي من نِیسْت — بلْکِه براي تُسْت — تا در شبِ تار سبُوي مرا نشِکنِي *

۳۲ شاعِري مِسْکِین پیشِ توَنگري رفْت و چُنان نزْدِیكِ او نِشسْت کِه مِیانِ شاعِر و توَنگر از یكْ وجب زِیاده تفاوُت نبُود * توَنگر ازِین سبب برْهم شُد و رُوي تُرش کرْد و پُرسید — کِه در مِیانِ تُو و خرچِه تفاوُت اسْت؟ گُفت بقدْرِ یكْ وجب * توَنگر ازِین جوَاب بِسْیار خجِل شُد و عُذْر نمُود *

۳۳ شخْصي با بخِیلي دوسْتِي داشْت * روزي بخِیل را گُفت کِه حالاً بسفر میروَم — انْگُشْترِيء خُود بمن بِدِه — آنرا با خُود خواهم داشْت — هرگاه اورا خواهم دِید تُرا یاد خواهم کرْد * جوَاب داد کِه اگر مرا یاد داشْتن مِیخواهِي — هرگاه انْگُشْتِ خُود خالِي بِینِي مرا یاد کُن — کِه انْگُشْترِي از فُلان خواسْته بُودم — نداد *

۳۴ شخْصي در خواب با شَیطان مُلاقات کرْد * یكْ سِیلِي بر رُوي او زد و رِیشِ اورا گرِفت و گُفت * اَي ملْعُون دُشْمنِ ما هسْتِي — و براي فریب دادنِ ما مرْدُمان رِیشِ دراز مِیدارِي * چُون سِیلِيُ دِیگر بر

رُوي او زد — بیدار شُد — و رِیشِ خُودرا در دستِ خُود دِید * شرمنده گردید — و بر خُود خندِید *

۳۵ پادشاهي دانشمندي‌را طلبید و گُفت — میخواهم که تُرا قاضيء این شهر کنم * دانشمند گُفت لایقِ اینکار نیَم * پادشاه پُرسید چرا * جَواب داد که آنچه گُفتم — اگر راست گُفتم — مرا معذُور دارید * و اگر دُروغ گُفتم — پس دُروغ‌گورا قاضِي کردن مصلحت نیست * پادشاه عُذرِ دانشمند پسندِید — و اورا معذُور داشت *

۳۶ دَرویشي تقصیرِ بُزُرگ کرد * پیشِ حبشِي کوتوال بُردند * کوتوال حُکم کرد که تمامِ رُوي دَرویش سِیاه کُنید — و در تمامِ شهر گردانید * دَرویش گُفت — اَي کوتوال نصفِ رُوي من سِیاه کُن — و گرنه همه مردُمانِ شهر خواهند دانست که حبشِي کوتوال هستم * کوتوال ازین سُخن خندِید — و تقصیرِ دَرویش مُعاف کرد *

۳۷ شخصي را به تُهمتِ زندقة و اِلحاد نزدِ هارُون اَلرّشِید آوردند — و او اِنکاري نمُود * هارُون الرّشید گُفت — هر آیِنه میزنم تا اِقرار کُني * آن مرد گُفت این خِلافِ حُکمِ خُداست * حق تعالِي فرمُوده است که تُو مردُمان را بِزني تا اِقرار بایِمان کُنند — و تُو مرا میزنِي که اِقرار بکُفر بِنمایم * هارُون بخندِید و اورا بخشِید *

۳۸ روزي شاعِري تقصِیري کرد * پادشاه جلّاد را فرمُود که رو بروي من اورا بکُش * لرزه در اندامِ شاعِر اُفتاد * ندِیمي اورا گُفت — این چه نامردِي و بیجگریست؟ مردان گاهي اینچُنین نمي ترسند * شاعِر گُفت — اَي ندِیم اگر تُو مردِي بِیا — بجاي من بِنشِین تا من

برخيزم * پادشاه اِين لطيفه پسنديد ــ و خنديد ــ و تقصيرِاو مُعاف فرمود *

۳۹ شخصي پيشِ يك نَويسنده رفت و گُفت ــ خطّي بِنَويس * گُفت پاي من درد ميكُند * آن شخص گُفت تُرا جائي فِرِستادن نميخواهم ــ كِه چُنين عُذر ميكُني * جوَاب داد كِه اين سُخنِ تُو راست است ــ ليكن هرگاه كِه براي كسي خطّ مي نِويسم ــ طلبيده مي شَوم براي خواندنِ آن ــ زيرا كِه ديگر شخص خطّ من خواندن نميتَوَاند *

۴۰ شخصي نزدِ طبيب رفت و گُفت ــ شِكَمِ من درد ميكُند ــ دَوَا كُن * طبيب پُرسيد ــ اِمروز چه خورده؟ گُفت نانِ سوخته * طبيب دَوَا در چشمِ او كردن خواست * آن شخص گُفت اَي طبيب دردِ شِكمرا با چشم چه نِسبت؟ حكيم گُفت اوّل تُرا دَوَاي چشم مي بايد كرد ــ زيرا كِه اگر چشمت دُرست بُودي ــ نانِ سوخته نميخُوردي *

۴۱ اعرابي شُتُر گُم كرده بُود * سوگند ميخورد كِه چُون بيابم ــ بيكدرم بِفروشم * چُون شُتُر يافت ــ از سوگندِ خُود پشيمان شُد * گُربه در گردنِ شُتُر آويخت ــ و بانگ زد ــ كِه شُتُر را بيكدرم ميفروشم ــ وگُربه بصد درم ــ امّا ازيكديگر جُدا نمي كُنم ونمي فروشم * شخصي درآنجا رسيد وگُفت چه ارزان بُود اگر اين شُتُر را اين قِلاده در گردن نبُودي؟

۴۲ پادشاهي در خواب ديد كِه تمامِ دندانهاي او اُفتاده اند *

از مُنجّمی تعبیرِ آن پُرسید * گُفت که اَولاد و اقارِبِ پادشاه همه رُو بُروی پادشاه خواهند مُرد * پادشاه در خشم شُد ـــ و مُنجّم را قید کرد * وَ مُنجّمِ دیگر را طلبید و تعبیرِ آن خواب پُرسید * عرض کرد که از همه اَولاد و اقارِب پادشاه زِیاده‌تر خواهد زِیست * پادشاه اِین نُکته پسندید و اِنعام داد *

۱۴۳ دُزدی در مقامِ شخصی برای دُزدیدنِ اسپ رفت * اِتّفاقاً گرِفتار شُد * صاحِبِ اسپ دُزد را گُفت ـــ اگر حِکمتِ دُزدیِ اسپ مرا بِنُمائی ـــ تُرا آزاد بِکُنم * دُزد قبول کرد ـــ و نزدِ اسپ رفت ـــ و رسنِ پایِ او کُشاد * بعد از آن لگام داد ـــ پس بر اسپ سوار شُد ـــ و تیز راند ـــ و گُفت ـــ بِبِین اِین طور دُزدی میکُنند * مردُمان هر چند که تعاقُبِ او کردند ـــ نیافتند *

۱۴۴ روزی مُرغی بر درختی نِشسته بُود * پادشاه اورا دید ـــ و با حاضِران گُفت که اِین را به تیر خواهم کُشت * تیر و کمان را گرِفت ـــ و تیر بر مُرغ انداخت ـــ و خطا کرد * مُرغ پرید * پادشاه بِسیار خجل گردید * شخصی برای دفعِ خجلت گُفتن گرِفت ـــ که پادشاه اگر اوّل مُرغ را کُشتن خواست ـــ کُشتن می تَوانِست ـــ لیکن بر جانِ او رحم کرد ـــ و قصداً خطا نمُود *

۱۴۵ شخصی با یکی شرط کرد که اگر بازی نَیابم یک اثارِ گوشت از اندامِ من بتراش * چُون بازی نَیافت مُدّعی ایفائ شرط خواست * او قبول نکرد * هر دو پیشِ قاضی رفتند ـــ قاضی مُدّعی را گُفت ـــ مُعاف کُن * قبُول نکرد * قاضی برهم شُد و فرمُود که بتراش ـــ

لیکن اگر اندك زیاده از اثار خواهي تراشید ـــ ترا سیاست خواهم نمود * مدّعي نتوانست * ناچار شده معاف کرد *

۴۶ شخصي خطّي مي نوشت * مردي بیگانه نزد او نشست و طرفِ خطّ میدید * آن شخص در خطّ نوشت که مردي بیگانه و احمق نزدِ من نشسته است ـــ و خطّرا میخواند ـــ ازاین سبب هیچ راز نمي نویسم * آن مرد گفت مرا احمق مي پنداري ـــ چرا راز نمي نویسي ـــ خطِ تو نخوانده ام * نویسنده گفت اگر خطِ من نخواندي ـــ چگونه معلوم کردي که چنین نوشته ام *

۴۷ دانشمندي مصاحبِ پادشاه بود * موي ریشِ خود میکند * روزي پادشاه اورا گفت که اگر بارِ دیگر موي ریش خواهي برکند ـــ بر تو سیاست خواهم نمود * بعدِ چند روز دانشمند کاري کرد که پادشاه بسیار بر او مهربان گردید ـــ و اورا گفت ـــ هرچه بخواهي ترا ببخشم * دانشمند گفت ـــ ریشِ من مرا ببخش دیگر هیچ نمي خواهم * پادشاه تبسّم کرد و گفت ـــ اگر خوشيء تو در همین است بخشیدم *

۴۸ امیر تیمور لنگ چون بهندوستان رسید و مطربان طلبید و گفت ـــ از بزرگان شنیده ام که دراین شهر مطربانِ کامل اند * مطربي نابینا پیشِ پادشاه حاضر شد و سرود آغاز کرد * پادشاه بسیار خوش گردید و نامِ او پرسید * گفت نامِ من دولت است * پادشاه گفت دولت هم کور میشود * او جواب داد که اگر دولت کور نبودي ـــ بخانهء لنگ نه آمدي * پادشاه این جواب پسندید و انعامِ بسیار باو داد *

۴۹ پادشاهي بر دُشمني فوج فرِستاد * آن فوج شِکست یافت * شخصي جلد نزدِ پادشاه آمد و خبر رسانید که فوجِ شُما فتح یافت * پادشاه بِسیار خوش شُد * بعد از دو روز خبرِ شِکست آمد * پادشاه بر آن شخص سِیاست کردن خواست * عرض کرد که اَي خُداوند لایِقِ سِیاست نَیم ــ زِیرا که دو روز شُمارا خُشنود کردم * چِرا مرا نا خوش مِیکُنید * پادشاه اِین لطیفه‌را پسندِید و اورا اِنعام فرمود *

۵۰ درویشي نزدِ خواجهٔ بخیلي آمد وگُفت ــ پدرِ من وتُو آدم است و مادر حوا‌ست ــ پس ما و شُما برادر باشیم * و تُرا اِین همه مال است ــ اگر مرا قِسمتِ برادرانه دِهي چه شود * خواجه غُلامِ خودرا گُفت که یك فُلوسِ سِیاه وَیرا دِه * گُفت اَي خواجه چِرا قِسمتِ سَویَت رِعایت نمیکُني * گُفت خاموش باش ــ اگر برادرانِ دیگر بِشنوند ــ اِین نِیز بتُو نمِي رسد *

۵۱ شخصي بِسیار مُفلِس بود ــ اسپي داشت ــ آنرا در اِصطبل بست ــ لیکن طرفي که سرِ اسپان مِیشود دُمِ او کرد ــ و منادِي درداد که ــ اَي مردُمان تماشاي عجب به بِینید که سرِ اسپ بجاي دُم است * همه مردُمانِ شهر جمع شُدند * هر شخصي که درونِ اِصطبل براي تماشا رفتن میخواست از او اندکي نقد مِیگرِفت و اورا راه مِیداد * هر که در آن اِصطبل مِیرفت شرمنده از آنجا باز مِي آمد ــ و هیچ نمِي گُفت *

۵۲ پادشاهي از مُنجمي پُرسید که چند سال از عُمرِ من باقِي است؟ گُفت ده سال * پادشاه بِسیار مُتفکِر گردِید و همچو بِیمار بر

بِستر اُفتاد * وزیر بِسیار عاقِل بود مُنجّم را رُو برُوی پادشاه طلبید و پُرسید ـــ که چند سالِ عُمرِ تُو باقِی است؟ گُفت بیست سال * وزِیر همان وقت از شمشیر مُنجّم را رُو برُوی پادشاه بقتل رسانید * پادشاه خُوشنُود گردید و حِکمتِ وزِیر پسندِید و باز سُخنِ هیچ مُنجّم نشُنِید *

۵۳ شاعِری پیشِ تَوَنگری رفت و بِسیار اورا سِتُود * تونگر خُوشنُود شُد و گُفت ـــ نزدِ من نقد نِیست ـــ لیکِن غلّه بِسیار است ـــ اگر فردا بِیائِی بِدِهم * شاعِر بخانهٔ خُود رفت و وقتِ فجر نزدِ تَوَنگر باز آمد * تَوَنگر پُرسِید چِرا آمدِی؟ گُفت دِیروز وعدهٔ دادنِ غلّه کردید ـــ ازین سبب آمده‌ام * تَوَنگر گُفت ـــ عجب احمق هستِی ـــ تُو از سُخن مرا خُوش کردِی ـــ من نِیز تُرا خُوش نمُودم ـــ حالا غلّه چِرا دِهم؟ شاعِر شرمنده شُده باز رفت *

۵۴ زنی مِیرفت ـــ مردی اورا دِید و دُنبالِ او روان شُد * زن پُرسِید که چِرا پسِ من مِی آئِی؟ گُفت بر تُو عاشِق شُده ام * زن گُفت بر من چه عاشِق شُدهٔ؟ خواهرِ من از من خُوبتر است ـــ پسِ من مِی آید ـــ بِرو و بر او عاشِق شو * مرد از آنجا برگشت و زنی بدصُورت دِید ـــ بِسیار ناخُوش گردید و باز نزدِ او رفت و گُفت ـــ چِرا دُروغ گُفتِی؟ زن گُفت تُو نِیز راست نگُفتِی ـــ اگر عاشِقِ من مِی بُودِی پیشِ دِیگری چِرا مِیرفتِی؟ مرد شرمنده شُد *

۵۵ روزی پادشاهی ظالِم تنها از شهر بیرُون رفت ـــ شخصی را زیرِ درختی نِشسته دِید ـــ پُرسِید که پادشاهِ این مُلک چگُونه است ـــ ظالِم یا عادِل؟ گُفت بِسیار ظالِم است * پادشاه گُفت مرا مِی

شِناسِي ؟ گُفْت نه * پادْشاه گُفْت منم سُلْطانِ اِین مُلْك * آن مرْد تَرْسید و پُرْسید ــ مرا مِیدانِي ؟ پادْشاه گُفْت نه * گُفْت پسرِ فُلان سَوداگرام ــ هرماه سِه روز دِیوانه مِیشَوم * اِمروزیکي ازآن سِه روز اسْت * پادْشاه خنْدِید و اورا هیچ نگُفْت *

۵۶ شخْصي هر روز شش نان مِیخرِید * روزي دوسْتي از وَي پُرْسید ــ شش نان‌را هر روز چه مِي کُنِي ؟ گُفْت نانيرا نِگاه مِیدارم و یك نان‌را مِي انْدازم و دُو نان‌را واپس مِیکُنم و دُو نان‌را قرْض مِیدِهم * آن دوسْت گُفْت سُخنِ تُو هیچ نِمي فهْمم صاف بِگو * گُفت یك نان کِه مِیدارم مِیخُورم ــ و نانيِ کِه مِي انْدازم خُوشدامن را مِیدِهم ــ و دُو نان کِه واپس مِیکُنم مادر و پدر را مِیدِهم ــ و دُو نان کِه قرْض مِیکُنم پسرانِ خُودرا مِیدِهم *

۵۷ دُو زن در طِفْلي مُنازعت مِیکرْدنْد و گَواه نداشْتنْد * هردُو پیشِ قاضِي رفْتنْد وانْصاف خواسْتنْد قاضِي جلّادرا طلبِید و فرمُود کِه اِین طِفْل‌را دُو پاره کُن و بهردُو زن بِدِه * زني چُون اِین سُخن شُنِید خاموش مانْد ــ و زنِ دِیگر شور و فرْیاد آغاز کرْد ــ کِه براي خُدا طِفْلِ مرا دُو نِیم مکُن ــ اگرچُنِین اِنْصاف اسْت طِفْل‌را نِمي خواهم * قاضِي بیَقِین پِنْداشْت کِه مادرِ طِفْل همِین اسْت * طِفْل باو سِپُرْد ــ وزنِ دِیگررا تازِیانه زده رانْد *

۵۸ شخْصي‌را یك کِیسهٔ دِینار در خانه گُم شُد * او بقاضِي خبر کرْد * قاضِي همه مرْدمانِ خانه را طلبِید و بهرکس یکْیك چوب داد ــ کِه همه آن در طُول برابر بُود ــ و گُفْت هرکِه دُزْد اسْت چوبِ

او بقدرِ یك انگشت دراز خواهد شد * چون همه‌را رخصت کرد شخصي که دزدیده بود ترسید و چوبِ خودرا بقدرِ یك انگشت تراشید * روزِ دیگر چون قاضي همه‌را طلبید و چوبها دید معلوم کرد که دزد کیست * کیسهٔ دینار از او گرفت وسیاست نمود *

۵۹ شبي قاضيء در کتابي دید که هرکه سرِ خورد میدارد و ریشِ دراز احمق میشود * قاضي سرِ خورد داشت و ریشِ بسیار دراز * با خود گفت که سررا بزرگ کردن نمیتوانم — لیکن ریش‌را کوتاه خواهم کرد * مقراض تلاش کرد نیافت — ناچار نیمِ ریش‌را در دست گرفت و نیم نزدِ چراغ برد * چون موي‌را آتش گرفت شعله بردستِ او رسید ریش‌را گذاشت * همه ریشِ او سوخته شد * قاضي بسیار شرمنده گردید به سببِ این که هرچه در کتاب بود باثبات رسید

۶۰ روزي سکندر با حاضران گفت که گاهي کسي‌را محروم نکردم هرکس هرچه از من خواست بخشیدم * شخصي آن وقت عرض کرد که خداوند مرا یکدرم درکار است بخش * سکندر فرمود که از پادشاهان چیزِ محقر خواستن بي‌ادبي است * آن شخص گفت که اگر پادشاه‌را از یکدرم دادن شرم مي آید ملکي مرا بخشد * سکندر گفت اول سوال کردي کم از مرتبهٔ من — و دیگر سوال کردي زیاده از مرتبهٔ خود * هر دو سوال بیجا کردي * آن شخص لا جواب و شرمنده گردید

۶۱ روزي باز خروسي‌را گفت — بسیار بیوفا هستي مردمان ترا مي پرورند و براي تو خانه مي سازند و هر گاه ترا گرفتن میخواهند چرا میگریزي ؟ من اگرچه مرغِ جنگلي ام لیکن چند روز که از دستِ

مَردُمان طُعمه میخورم برای ایشان شِکار میکُنم — و هرچند دُور میروم چُون طلبیده میشوم بازمی آیم * خُروس جواب داد که گاهی بازیرا برسیخ دیده؟ و من بِسیار خُروسان‌را برسیخ کباب و برآتش بریان دیده‌ام * تو بِسیار دُور گُریزی اگر بازیرا برسیخ بِبینی * باز لا جواب شُد *

۶۲ پادشاهی از مسخره برنجید — و زیرِ پای فیل انداختن فرمود * مسخره شور نمود که ای خُداوند — منِ ضعیف لائقِ پای فیل نیستم — مرا زیرِ پای صعوه انداز — و زیرِ پای فیل وزیررا — زیرا که وزیر فربه است اُستخوانهای او در پای فیل بخواهند خلید * پادشاه طرفِ وزیر دید و تبسّم کرد و گُفت — چه میگوئی؟ وزیر عرض کرد که برای خُدا تقصیرِ این حرامزاده بِبخش — وگرنه مرا نیز در بلا خواهد انداخت * پادشاه‌را سُخنِ مسخره و شفاعتِ وزیر پسند آمد * تقصیر مُعاف کرد و خلعت بخشید *

۶۳ شخصی نوکرِ خودرا گُفت که علی الصّباح اگر دُو زاغ‌را یکجا نِشسته بِبینی مرا خبر کُن که آنهارا خواهم دید و شُگونِ نیک خواهم یافت * تمام روز مرا بخوشی خواهد گُذشت القصّه نوکرِ او دُو زاغ‌را یکجا دید * صاحبِ خُودرا خبر داد * صاحبِ او چُون بیرون آمد یک زاغ‌را دید — دیگر زاغ پریده بُود * بِسیار بر نوکر غُصّه شُد و تازیانه زدن گرفت * همان وقت دوستی برای او طعام فرستاد * نوکر عرض کرد که ای خُداوند — یک زاغ‌را دیدی طعام یافتی — اگر دُو زاغ‌را میدیدی می یافتی آنچه من یافتم

٦۴ دُو مُصَوِّر باهم گُفتند كه ما هر دُو كسان تصوير بكشيم بِه بينيم كُدام خُوب ميكشد * يك مُصَوِّر خوشهء انگور نقش نمود و آنرا بر دروازه آويخت * مُرغان آمدند و بر آن منقار زدند * مردمان آن تصوير را بِسيار پسنديدند و در خانهء مُصَوِّرِ ديگر رفتند و پرسيدند كه كُجا تصوير كشيدهء ؟ — گُفت در پسِ اين پرده * مُصَوِّرِ اوّل خواست كه پرده بردارد چون دست بر پرده نِهاد معلوم كرد كه پرده نيست — بلكه ديوار است كه بر آن تصوير كشيده است * مُصَوِّرِ ثانِي گُفت كه تُو چُنان تصوير كشيدي كه مُرغان فريفتند — و من چُنان تصوير كشيدم كه مُصَوِّر فريفت *

٦٥ شخصي يك طُوطي پرورد — و اورا زبانِ پارسي آموخت * طُوطي در جوابِ هر سُخن مي گُفت — دراين چه شكّ * روزي آن شخص طُوطي را در بازار براي فروختن بُرد و صد رُوپيه قيمتِ آن ظاهر كرد * مُغلي از طُوطي پرسيد كه لائقِ صد رُوپيه هستي؟ گُفت — در اين چه شكّ * مُغل خُوشنُود شُد و طُوطي را خريد وبخانهء خُود بُرد * هر سُخن كه با طُوطي ميگُفت جوابِ آن — دراين چه شكّ — ميافت * در دلِ خُود شرمنده و پشيمان گرديد و گُفته حِماقت كردم كه چُنين طُوطي خريدم * گُفت — دراين چه شكّ * مُغل را تبسّم آمد و طُوطي را آزاد كرد *

٦٦ دانشمندي در مسجد مي نشست و با مردمان وعظ مي گُفت * شخصي در آن مجلس هر روز مي گريست * روزي دانشمند گُفت كه سُخنِ من در دلِ اين شخص بِسيار اثر ميكُند ازين سبب ميگريد *

دِیگران آن شخص‌را گُفتند کِه در دِلِ ما سُخنِ دانِشمند هیچ اثر نمیکند
چگونهء دِل دارِي کـه میگرِئِي ؟ گُفت بـر سُخنِ دانِشمند نمِیگرِیم —
بلکِه یك خصِي پرورده بُودم و اورا بِسیار دوست داشتم — چون
خصِي پِیر شُد مُرد — هرگاه دانِشمند سُخن مِیگوید و رِیشِ او مِي
جُنبد خصِي مرا یاد مِي آید — زِیرا کِه او هم اِینچنِین رِیشِ دراز داشت *

٦٧ روزِي امِیرِي بر میخ تِیر مِي انداخت * تِیراندازانِ بِسیار آنجا
حاضِر بُودند * تِیرِ کسِي بر میخ نمیرسید * فقِیرِي آنجا رفت و از امِیر
چِیزِي سُؤال کرد * امِیر تِیر و کمانِ خُود در دستِ فقِیر داد و فرمُود —
میخ‌را بِزن * فقِیر تِیر بر میخ پرتاب کرد — اِتِّفاقًا بزد * امِیر بِسیار
خُوشنُود گردید و صد رُوپیه فقِیررا بخشِید و رخصت کرد * فقِیر امِیررا
گُفت — سُؤال کردم — هیچ نیافتم * امِیر رُوي درهم کشِید و گُفت
صد رُوپِیه تُرا بخشِیده‌ام — میگوئِي هیچ نیافتم ؟ — این چِه سُخن
است ؟ فقِیر گُفت صد رُوپِیه میخ زده گرِفتم — و از سُؤال چِه یافتم ؟
امِیر خندِید و اِنعامِ دِیگر هم بخشِید *

٦٨ درویشِي بر دُوکانِ بقّالِي رفت — و در خرِیدن شِتابِي کرد *
بقّال درویش‌را دُشنام داد * درویش در خشم شُد و پاپوشِي بر سرِ بقّال
زد * بقّال پیشِ کوتوال رفت و نالِش نمُود * کوتوال درویشرا طلبِید
و پُرسید کِه چِرا بقّال‌را زدِي ؟ درویش گُفت کِه بقّال مرا دُشنام داد *
کوتوال گُفت — اَي درویش تقصِیرِ بُزُرگ کردِي — لیکِن فقِیر هستِي
ازِین سبب تُرا سِیاست نمِي کُنم * بِرَو هشت آنه ببقّال بِدِه کِه
سزاي تقصِیرِ تُو همِین است * درویش یکرُوپِیه از جیبِ خُود بر آورد

D

و در دستِ کوتوال داد — و یك پاپوش بر سرِ کوتوال زد و گفت — اگر چنین اِنصاف است — هشت آنه تو بِگیر — و هشت آنه آنرا بِدِه *

۶۹ غُلامي از نزدِ صاحِبِ خود گریخت * بعدِ چند روز صاحِبِ او در شهرِ دیگر رفت * آنجا غُلام‌را دِید و اورا گِرِفت و گفت — چرا گریختي ؟ غُلام دست در دامنِ خواجه زده گفت — غُلامِ من هستي نقدِ بِسیار از من دُزدیدي و گریختي — حالاً که تُرا یافته ام — بر تُو سِیاست خواهم نمود * القصّه هردُو پیشِ قاضي رفتند و اِنصاف خواستند * قاضِي آن هر دُورا نزدِ دریچه اِستاده کرد و فرمود که بیکبار هردُو از دریچه سرها بیرون کُنید * چون سر بیرون کردند قاضِي جلّادرا فرمود که شمشیر بر سرِ غُلام بِزن * غُلام چون این سخن بشنید در حال سرِ خود اندرون کشید — وصاحِبِ او اصلاً مُجنبید * قاضِي غُلام‌را سِیاست کرد — و بصاحِبِ او سِپرد *

۷۰ روزي اِبراهِیم ادهم بر درِ سرایِ خویش نِشسته بُود و غُلامان نزدِ او صفّ زده * ناگاه درویشي درآمد — با دلقي وانباني و عصائي * خواست که در سرایِ اِبراهِیم رود * غُلامان گفتند اَي پیر کجا مي روي * پیر گفت درین خان مي روم * گفتند این خانهٔ پادشاهِ بلخست نه خان * اِبراهیم فرمود تا اورا پیش آوردند — گفت اَي درویش این سراي منست * پیر گفت اَي اِبراهیم این خانه اوّل ازانِ که بوده است ؟ گفت ازآنِ جدّم * گفت چون او در گذشت ازانِ که شُد ؟ گفت ازانِ پدم * گفت چون پدرت بمرد ازانِ که شُد ؟ گفت ازانِ

من * گفت چون تو بمیری کِرا باشد؟ گُفت پِسرِ مرا * گُفت اَي اِبراهیم جائی که یکي در مي رَوَد ویکي بیرون مي آید خاني باشد نه سوای *

۷۱ بخیلي دوستي‌را گفت یك هزار روپیه نزدِ من است مي خواهم که این روپیه‌هارا بیرون از شهر دفن کنم — و سِوای تو با کسي این راز نگویم * القصّه هر دو کسان بیرونِ شهر رفته زیرِ درختي نقدِ مذکوررا دفن کردند * بعدِ چند روز بخیل تنها زیرِ آن درخت رفت — از نقد هیچ نشان نیافت * با خود گفت که سِوای آن دوست کسي دیگر نبود — لیکن اگر ازاو بپرسم هرگز اقرار نخواهد کرد * پس بخانهٔ او رفت و گفت — بسیار نقد بدستِ من آمده است — مي خواهم که همانجا نهیم لیکن اگر فردا بیائي با هم برویم * دوستِ مذکور بطمعِ نقدِ بسیار آن نقدرا آنجا باز نهاد * بخیل روزِ دیگر آنجا تنها رفت — نقدِ خود یافت — حکمتِ خودرا پسندید و باز بر دوستيِ دوستان اعتماد نکرد *

۷۲ زني پیشِ قاضي رفت و گفت که فلان مرد با من بزور زِنا کرد * قاضي آن مردرا طلبید و پرسید که چرا آبروي این زن ریختي؟ مرد انکار کرد * قاضي فرمود که ده روپیه جرمانه باین زن بده * مرد ناچار بموجبِ حکمِ قاضي زر بزن داد * چون زن بیرون رفت قاضي مردرا فرمود — بِرَو و نقد خود از زن باز گیر * مرد چون این حکم یافت دَوید — و هرچند خواست که روپیه از زن بزور بگیرد نتوانست * زن پیشِ قاضي باز آمد و عرض کرد که آن مرد روپیه از من بزور میگیرد

هنوز نداده ام — اگر مرضیء حضرت است بدهم * قاضي گفت مرد که نقدرا بزور از تو گرفتن نتوانست — بي رضاي تو چگونه با تو زنا کرد ؟ تو دروغ گوئي — برو و نقد باو بسپار و باز اینچنین اِفتِرا مکن *

۷۳ دو کس مالِ خود پیر زنيرا سپردند و گفتند — که هرگاه ما هردو خواهیم آمد خواهیم گرفت * بعدِ چند روز شخصي از آنها نزدِ زن آمد و گفت — شریکِ من مُرد — حالاً مال مرا بده * پیر زن ناچار شد و داد * پسِ چند روز شخصِ دیگر آمد و مال خواست * زن گفت که شریکِ تو آمده بُود و ترا مُرده ظاهر ساخت — هر چند مبالغه کردم لیکن سخن من نشنید و همه مالرا بُرد * شخصِ مذکور زنرا پیشِ قاضي بُرد و انصاف خواست * قاضي بعد از تامّل دریافت که زن بي تقصیر است — فرمود که تو اوّل شرط کرده بودي که هرگاه ما هردو شریک خواهیم آمد مال خواهیم گرفت * تو شریکِ خودرا بیار و مال بگیرید — تنها چگونه بیايي ؟ مرد لا جواب شده راهِ خود پیش گرفت *

۷۴ در شهري انبارِ پُنبه بدُزدي رفت * پنبه‌فروشان شِکایت به پادشاه بردند * پادشاه هرچند که تجسّس فرمود دزديرا نیافت * امیري عرض کرد که اگر فرمان باشد دزدانرا بگیرم * پادشاه حکم داد * امیر بخانهء خود رفت و خورد و بزرگِ شهررا ببهانهء ضیافت طلبید * چون همه مردمان جمع شدند و نشستند امیر درآن مجلس رفت و بر روي همه مردمان نظر کرد و گفت — چه حرامزاده و بیحیا و احمق

مردمان اند که پُنبه دزدیده اند ؟ و ریزهاي پُنبه در ریشهاي ایشان جا کرده است ـــ ودر مجلس من آمده اند * چند کس همان وقت ریشهاي خودرا از دست پاك کردند ـــ و معلوم شد که آنها دزدان اند * پادشاه بر حکمتِ امیر آفرین و تحسین نمود *

۷۵ پادشاهي در جنگ شکست یافت ـــ شخصي از فوجِ دشمن اورا گرفت و نشناخت که پادشاه است ـــ اسبابِ خود بر سرِ او نهاد * چون بمنزل رسید قدري برنج اورا داد که بپز و بخور * پادشاه بسیار گُرسنه بود برنج را در سبو کرد و بر آتش نهاد و خود از آتش دور نشست * سگي آمد و سبورا گرفت و گریخت ـــ پادشاه خندید * آن شخص بر پادشاه غُصّه شد و گفت ـــ اي احمق سگ سبوي ترا بُرد و خنده کردي ـــ بگو سبب چیست ؟ پادشاه خاموش ماند * چون تازیانه یافت گفت روزي چنان بودم که هرگاه براي شکار میرفتم صد شتر اسبابِ باورچیخانهء من همراه میرفت * اِمروز چنان هستم که مُشت برنج هم سگ نگذاشت * آن شخص عذر تقصیرات نمود و گذاشت *

۷۶ سوداگران پیشِ پادشاهي رفتند و اسپانرا براو عرض نمودند * پادشاه بسیار پسندید و خرید و دو لك روپیه زیاده از قیمت بسوداگران داد و فرمود ـــ که از مُلکِ خود باز اسپانرا بیارید * سوداگران رخصت شدند * روزي پادشاه در حالتِ خوشي و مستي وزیررا گفت که اسامیء جمیع احمقان بنویس * وزیر عرض کرد که پیش ازین نوشته ام و اوّلِ نامها نامِ حضرتست * پرسید چرا ؟ گفت سوداگران را دو لك روپیه که براي آوردنِ اسپان بي ضامني و اِطّلاعِ مساکنِ انها

عنایت شد ـــ علامت حماقت است * پادشاه گفت اگر سوداگران اسپان‌را بیارند پس چه باید کرد؟ گفت اگر بیارند نامِ حضرت از دفترِ احمقان محو خواهم کرد و نامِ سوداگران آنجا خواهم نوشت *

۷۷ دانشمندي در شهري رفت ـــ شنید که در این شهر شخصي سخاوتِ بسیار میدارد و مسافرانرا طعام میدهد * دانشمند با پارچهٔ کهنه و کثیفه پیشِ او رفت * آن شخص هیچ التفات نکرد و جاي نشستن نداد * دانشمند شرمنده شد و باز آمد * روزِ دیگر پارچهٔ پاکیزه بکرایه گرفت و پوشیده پیشِ او رفت * صاحبِ خانه تعظیمِ او کرد و نزدِ خود نشانید و طعامِ لذیذ براي او خواست * دانشمند چون بر طعام نشست لقمه در پارچهٔ خود نهادن گرفت * صاحبِ خانه پرسید چرا این چنین میکني؟ گفت دیروز با پارچهٔ کهنه آمده بودم هیچ طعام نیافتم ـــ امروز که پارچهٔ خوب دارم مي پندارم که این طعام براي پارچه است نه براي من * آن شخص شرمنده گردید و عذر نمود *

۷۸ پادشاهي آهنگري‌را فرمود که جوشنئ خوب براي من تیّار کن * آهنگر تیّار کرده پیشِ پادشاه برد * پادشاه بقصدِ آزمودن جوشن‌را بر زمین نهاد و شمشیر بر آن زد ـــ دو نیم شد * آهنگررا فرمود که اگر باز چنین جوشن خواهي ساخت سرِ تو دو نیم خواهم کرد * آهنگر بخانهٔ خود رفت * دختري داشت ـــ با او این احوال گفت * دختر اورا مصلحت داد که باز جوشن بساز * این بار من پیشِ پادشاه خواهم برد * القصّه آهنگر جوشن‌را ساخت * دخترِ او آن جوشن‌را پوشید و

شمشیري در دست گرفت و پیشِ پادشاه رفت و عرض کرد که حالاً جوشن را بیازمائید * پادشاه گفت چرا این را پوشیدهٔ * گفت اي خداوند دستور آن است که جوشن بر اندام آزموده میشود ازاین سبب پوشیده‌ام * پادشاه این سخن پسندید و اورا انعام بخشید *

۷۹ جماعتي نزدِ قاضي قرضدارِ خود را آوردند وگفتند که این مرد از ما هزار دینار قرض گرفته است ونمیدهد * قاضي باو گفت که چه میگوئي * گفت ایشان راست میگویند ودعويء ایشان حقّ است * غایتش اینکه این مقدارِ فُرصت از ایشان میخواهم که گلهٔ شترهاي خود را بفروشم وباغها را گِرْو کنم وحقِّ ایشان را ادا سازم * آن جماعت گفتند واللّه سراپا دروغ میگوید مالکِ یك دینار نیست ویك وجبِ زمین در مِلك خود ندارد مالکِ یك گوسفند نیست چه جاي گلهٔ شتران * قرضدار جواب داد که اي عدالت‌پناه اکنون اقرارِ ایشان بمفلسي وبیچیزيء من استمع نمودي پس چگونه از مفلس چیزي طلب مي نمایند * قاضي رو به ایشان کرد وگفت اَلْمُفْلِسُ فِي اَمَانِ اللّٰهِ واورا از دستِ آنها خلاص کرد *

۸۰ شخصي پیش پادشاهي رفت و عرض کرد که مردي همیشه در خانهٔ من مي آید و با زنِ من دوستي دارد لیکن گاهي اورا نمي بینم و نمیدانم که کیست میخواهم که گرفتارش کنم ازحضرت امّیدوارِ انصاف ام * پادشاه شیشهٔ عِطْر باو داد و فرمود که بزنِ خود سِپار و بگو که کسي را مدِه * آن شخص همچنان کرد * پادشاه جاسوسِ چندرا بر گماشت که گِردِ خانهٔ او بنشینند و از پارچهٔ هرکسي که بوي عِطْر

آید اورا گرفته بیارند * القصّه حریف قابو یافته نزدِ زن رفت * زن عِطْررا درپارچهء او مالید و گفت که شوهرِ من اگرچه مرا فرمود که کسيرا این عطر مدِه لیکن تو که جان و دلِ مني اگر بکارت نیاید بچه کار آید * چون حریف از آن جا بر آمد جاسوسان ببوي عطر سر راهش گرفتند و اسیر کرده پیشِ پادشاه بُردند * پادشاه آن شخصرا طلبید و گفت حریفِ زنِ تو حاضر است اورا ببر و بکُش یا ببخش *

۸۱ زني با زنِ همسایهء خود دشمني داشت * شبي مَيء بسیار خورد و مست شد و طفلِ خودرا کُشت و در خانهء زنِ همسایه انداخت و صباح برو تهمت نهاد که طفلِ مرا کشته است و اورا پیش قاضي برد * قاضي اوّل زنِ همسایهرا در خلوت طلبید و بسیار ترسانید و گفت راست بگو و گرنه ترا خواهم کُشت * زن قسم خورد و انکار کرد * قاضي گفت که اگر روبروي من برهنه شوي سخنِ تو راست پندارم * زن از حیا سر فرو کرد و گفت مرا کشته شدن قبول است لیکن زنهار برهنه نخواهم شد * قاضي اورا رخصت کرد و زنِ فریاديرا در خلوت طلبید و گفت اگر پیشِ من برهنه شوي سخن تو باور کنم * آن زن خواست که خودرا برهنه کند * قاضي اورا منع کرد و گفت که پسررا خود کشتي * چون چند تازیانه اورا زد اقرار کرد که خود تقصیر کردم و تهمت برو نهادم * القصّه قاضي اورا بر دار کشید *

۸۲ شخصي گرسنه میرفت اعرابيرا دید که بر کنارهء برِکه طعام میخورد * نزدِ او رفت و گفت از طرفِ خانهء تو مي آیم * اعرابي پرسید که زن و فرزند و شترِ من همه بخیریَت اند * گفت بلي * اعرابيرا

خاطر جمع شد و باز بران شخص نظر نکرد * آن شخص آغاز کرد که ای اعرابی این سگ که حالاً بحضورِ تو نشسته است اگر سگِ تو زنده میماند چنین میشد * اعرابی سر بالا کرد و گفت سگِ من از چه سبب مُرد * گفت گوشتِ شترِ تو بسیار خورد * پرسید شتر چگونه مُرد * گفت زنِ تو مُرد ازین سبب کسی اورا کاه و دانه و آب نداد * پرسید زن چگونه مُرد گفت در غمِ پسرِ تو بسیار گریست و سنگ بر سر و سینه زد * پرسید پسر چگونه مُرد گفت خانه برو اُفتاد * اعرابی چون این احوالِ خانه‌خرابی شنید خاك برسر انداخت و طعام‌را همانجا گذاشت و طرفِ خانهٔ خود روانه شد * آن شخص بدین حکمت طعام یافت *

۸۳ روزی پادشاهی با وزیر برای سَیر رفت بکِشت‌زاری رسید درختانِ گندم دید از قدِ آدم درازتر * پادشاه متعجّب شد و گفت چنین دراز درختانِ گندم گاهی ندیدم * وزیر عرض کرد که ای خداوند در وطنِ من درختانِ گندم همچو قدِ فیل بلند میشوند * پادشاه تبسّم نمود * وزیر با خود گفت که پادشاه سخنِ من دروغ پنداشت ازین سبب تبسّم کرد * چون از سَیر باز آمد خطّ بمردمانِ وطنِ خود برای چند درختانِ گندم فرستاد * تا که خطّ آنجا رسید فصلِ گندم گذشته بود * القصّه بعدِ یکسال درختانِ گندم از آنجا رسیدند * وزیر پیشِ پادشاه بُرد * پادشاه پرسید چرا آوردی * عرض کرد که در سالِ گذشته روزی عرض کرده بودم که درختانِ گندم همچو قدِ فیل بلند می شوند تبسّم کردید * با خود گفتم که سخنِ من دروغ پنداشتند * برای تصدیقِ سخنِ خود آوردم * پادشاه گفت حالاً باور

کردم لیکن زنهار پیشِ کسي چنین سخن مگو که بعدِ سالي باور کند *

۸۴ روزي پادشاهي بر بامِ قصرِ خود نشسته بود * شخصي را زیرِ دیوار استاده دید که مرغي در دست گرفته مي نمود * پادشاه اورا طلبید و پرسید چرا مرغ بمن مي نمائي * گفت اي خداوند با شخصي از طرفِ حضرت شرط کردم و این مرغ در بازي یافتم براي خداوند آورده ام * پادشاه خوشنود گردید و مرغ را در مطبخ فرستاد * بعد از دو سه روز باز آن شخص پیشِ پادشاه آمد و گوسپندي آورد و گفت این هم از نام آنحضرت در بازي یافته ام * پادشاه آنرا نیز قبول کرد * سیوم بار پیشِ بادشاه رفت و شخصي دیگررا با خود برد * چون بادشاه اورا تهیدست دید پرسید براي من هیچ نه آوردهٔ * عرض کرد که از طرفِ حضرت با این شخص دو هزار روپیه را شرط نمودم و بازي نیافتم حالاً این شخص براي زر پیشِ حضرت آمده است * پادشاه تبسّم کرد و زر اورا بخشید و فرمود گاهي از طرفِ من با کسي قِمار مباز * دیگر هیچ از تو نخواهم گرفت و نه ترا چیزي خواهم داد *

۸۵ آورده اند که سلطان محمود ایّاز را بسیار دوست داشتي ازین سبب همه ارکانِ دَولت برو حسد بردند و پادشاه را گفتند که ایّاز هر روز تنها به جَوَاهرخانه میرود ومعلوم میشود که چیزي مي دُزدد وگرنه در جَوَاهرخانه اورا چه کار است * پادشاه گفت هرگاه بچشمِ خود خواهم دید باور خواهم کرد * روزِ دیگر پادشاه را خبر دادند که ایّاز تنها در جواهرخانه رفته است پادشاه از غرفه درونِ جواهرخانه نظر کرد چه مي بیند که ایّاز صندوقي را گشاده پارچهٔ کهنه وغلیظ پوشیده است *

پادشاه درون تشریف برد پرسید چرا چنین پارچه پوشیدهٔ * عرض کرد که اي خداوند چون در بندگيء حضرت نبودم چنین پارچه داشتم حالا که بدولتِ خداوند پارچه‌هاي پاکیزه دارم جامهٔ کهنهٔ خود هر روز مي بینم و مي پوشم تا حالتِ قدیمِ خود را فراموش نکنم وقدرِ نعمتِ خداوندي شناسم * پادشاه چون این جواب شنید پسندید واورا درکنارِ کشید ومرتبهٔ او بزرگ کرد *

۸۶ شخصي مالِ بسیار صرّافي‌را سپرد و بسفر رفت * چون باز آمد تقاضا نمود * صرّاف انکار کرد و قسم خورد که مرا نه سپردهٔ * آن شخص پیشِ قاضي رفت و احوالِ خود گفت * قاضي تأمّل کرد و فرمود کس‌را مگو که فلان صرّاف مالِ تو نمیدهد تدبیري براي مالِ تو خواهم کرد * روزِ دیگر قاضي آن صرّاف‌را طلبید و گفت کارهاي بسیار بمن پیش آمده است تنها کردن نمیتوانم ترا نائبِ خود کردن میخواهم زیرا که مُتَدَیِّن هستي * صراف قبول کرد و بسیار خوش گردید * چون بخانه رفت قاضي آن شخص‌را طلبید و گفت حالا مالِ خود از صرّاف بخواه البتّه خواهد داد * شخصِ مذکور پیشِ صرّاف رفت وصرّاف چون روي او دید گفت بیا بیا خوش‌آمدي مالِ تو فراموش کرده بودم دِي شب مرا یاد آمد * القِصّه مال باو داد و از طَمعِ نیابت پیشِ قاضي رفت * قاضي گفت اِمروز پیشِ پادشاه رفته بودم شنیدم که کاري بزرگ ترا سپردن میخواهد خدارا شکر کن مرتبهٔ بزرگ خواهي یافت حالا نائبِ دیگر براي خود تلاش خواهم کرد * القِصّه قاضي اورا بدین حیله رخصت کرد *

۸۷ سواري در شهري رفت شنید که اینجا دزدان بسیار اند * وقتِ شب سائس‌را گفت که تو بِخُسپ من بیدار خواهم ماند زیرا که مرا بر تو اعتماد نیست * سائِس گفت اي خداوند این چه سخن است نمي پسندم که من در خواب باشم و صاحب بیدار زنهار اینچنین نخواهم کرد * القصّه صاحبِ او خفت و بعدِ یکپاس بیدار گردید سائِس‌را گفت چه میکني * گفت در فکر هستم که خدا زمین‌را برآب چگونه گسترد * گفت میترسم که دزدان آیند و ترا خبر نشود * گفت اي خداوند خاطر جمع دارید خبردار هستم * سوار باز خفت و نصف شب بیدار شد و پرسید اي سائس چه میکني * گفت در فکرم که خدا آسمانرا چگونه بي ستون استاده کرد * گفت در فکرِ تو میترسم مبادا که دزدان اسپ‌را برند * گفت اي خداوند بیدار هستم چگونه دزدان خواهند آمد * سوار گفت اگر خفتن میخواهي بخسپ من بیدار خواهم ماند * گفت مرا خواب نمي آید * سوار باز خفت و چون ساعتي شب باقي ماند بیدار شد سائِس‌را پرسید چه میکني * گفت در فکر هستم که اسپ‌را دزد برده است و فردا زین‌را من بر سر خواهم برداشت یا صاحب *

۸۸ پادشاهي را وزیرِ عاقل بود دست از وزارت برداشت وبعبادتِ خدا مشغول شد * پادشاه از امیران پرسید که وزیر کجا است * عرض کردند که از وزارت دست برداشته بعبادتِ الهي مشغول است * پادشاه پیشِ وزیر رفت وپرسید اي وزیر از من چه خطا دیدي که وزارت را ترك نمودي * گفت از پنج سبب اول آنکه تو نشسته مي

بودي ومن بحضور تو استاده میماندم اکنون بندگيء خدا میکنم که در وقتِ نماز مرا حکمِ نشستن داده است * دوم آنکه تو طعام مي خوردي و من نگاه میکردم اکنون رزّاقي پیدا کرده ام که او نمي خورد و مرا مي خوراند * سیوم آنکه تو خواب میکردي ومن پاسباني میکردم اکنون خداي دارم که من خواب میکنم و او پاسبانيء من میکند * چهارم آنکه همیشه مي ترسیدم که اگر تو بمیري مرا از دشمنان آسیب برسد اکنون چنان خداي دارم که نخواهد مرد ومرا از دشمنان هیچ آسیب نخواهد رسید * پنجم آنکه از تو مي ترسیدم که اگر از من گناهي شود عفو نکني اکنون خداي من چنان رحیم است که هر روز صد گناه میکنم و او مي بخشد *

۸۹ ماهي‌گیري همیشه ماهیانِ دریا گرفتي و در بازار فروختي * روزي یك ماهيء زنده گرفت و آنچنان خوب گاهي نگرفته بود در دلِ خود گفت که اگر این ماهي را در بازار بفروشم زیاده از دو سه فلوس نخواهم یافت مصلحت آنست که پیشِ پادشاه برم البتّه بسیار انعام خواهد داد * القصّه ماهي را پیشِ پادشاه بُرد * پادشاه چون ماهي‌را دید بسیار پسندید و خوشنود شد و حکم کرد که ماهي‌گیررا صد روپیه دهند * وزیر آن وقت حاضر بود در گوشِ پادشاه عرض کرد که براي یك ماهي اینقدر نقد دادن مصلحت نیست * پادشاه جواب داد که اگر ندهم جاي شرم است زیرا که حالاً حکم کرده‌ام * وزیر گفت مصلحت آن است که از ماهي‌گیر بپرسید که این ماهي نر است یا ماده * اگر بگوید که نر است ماده‌را بخواهید اگر بگوید ماده است نررا بخواهید *

ماهي‌گیر مثلِ آن آوردن نخواهد توانست پس انعام هم نخواهد یافت * پادشاه سخنِ وزیر پسندید و از ماهي‌گیر پرسید که این ماهي نراست یا ماده ؟ ماهي‌گیر جواب داد که این ماهي خُنثي است * پادشاه بسیار خندید و دو صد روپیه اورا بخشید *

۹۰ شخصي پیشِ درویشي رفت و سه سوال کرد * اوّل آنکه چرا میگوئي که خدا همه جا حاضراست هیچ جا نمي بینم بنما کجاست * دوم آنکه انسان‌را براي تقصیري چرا سیاست میکنند هرچه میکند خدا میکند انسان‌را هیچ قدرت نیست و بي ارادتِ خدا هیچ نمي تواند کرد و اگر انسان‌را قدرت بودي همه کارها براي خود بهتر کردي * سیوم آنکه خدا شَیطان‌را در آتشِ دوزخ چگونه عقوبت تواند کرد زیرا که سرشتِ او از آتش است وآتش در آتش چه اثر خواهد کرد * درویش کلُوخي بزرگ بر سرِ او زد * آن شخص گریان پیشِ قاضي رفت و گفت از فلان درویش سه سوال کردم بر سرِ من چنان کلُوخي زد که سرِ من درد میکند و هیچ جواب نداد * قاضي درویش‌را طلبید و گفت چرا کلُوخ برسرِ او زدي و جوابِ سوالِ او ندادي ؟ درویش گفت که آن کلُوخ جوابِ سخنِ اوست میگوید که درد در سر دارد بنماید کجا است تا من خدارا باو بنمایم * و چرا پیشِ حضرت نالشِ من نمود هرچه کردم خدا کرد بي ارادتِ خدا اورا نزدم مرا چه قدرت است ؟ وسرشتِ او از خاك است از خاك چگونه اورا رنج رسید ؟ آن شخص شرمنده گردید قاضي جوابِ دروش بسیار پسندید *

۹۱ شخصي پیشِ پادشاه رفت و گفت دي شب مردي از فوجِ

پادشاهي بزور درخانهٔ من آمد و با کنیزِ من زنا کرد * پادشاه فرمود که اگر آن مرد باز در خانهٔ تو بیاید همان‌دم مرا خبرکن * شبِ دوم آن مرد باز آمد و در خانهٔ او رفت * صاحبِ خانه پادشاه‌را خبرداد * پادشاه شمشیري در دست گرفت و با اوروان شد * چون بخانهٔ او رسید اوّل چراغ را کُشت و بعدِ آن آن مردرا بقتل رسانید و باز چراغ را طلبید و روي آن مرد دید و خدارا شکرکرد وصاحبِ خانه‌را گفت هر طعام که این وقت درخانهٔ تو موجود باشد بیار* صاحبِ خانه طعام آورد پادشاه بسیار بخوشي خورد * صاحبِ خانه پرسید که اي خداوند بچه سبب اوّل چراغ‌را کشتید بعد از آن آنمردرا بقتل رسانید و چون روي آن مرد دیدید خدارا شکرکردید و طعام بیوقت خوردید ؟ پادشاه فرمود که پنداشته بودم که سواي پسرِ من کسي‌را چنین قدرت نیست ازاین سبب اوّل چراغ را کشتم که اگر روي پسر خواهم دید از شفقت اورا کشتن نخواهم توانست * چون کشته شد چراغ طلبیدم و روي او دیدم و خدارا شکرکردم که پسرِ من نیست * و آن وقت که از من انصاف خواستي باخود گفتم که تا آنمردرا نکشم هیچ نخورم * از آن وقت هیچ نخورده بودم ازاین سبب سخت گرسنه بودم و طعام بي وقت خوردم *

۹۲ دانشمندي هزار روپیه عطّاري را سپرد و بسفر رفت * بعدِ مدّت از سفر باز آمد و روپیه‌از عطّار خواست * عطّار گفت دروغ میگوئي مرا نه سپردهٔ * دانشمند باوي درآویخت * مردمان جمع شدند و دانشمندرا تکذیب کردند وگفتند این عطّار بسیار دیانت‌دار

است گاهي خیانت نکرد اگر با این مناقشه خواهي کرد سزا خواهي یافت * دانشمند ناچار شد و احوال بر کاغذي نوشت و پادشاه‌را نمود * پادشاه فرمود بِرَو نزدِ دوکانِ عطّار سه روز بنشین و اورا هیچ مگو چهارم روز آن طرف خواهم رفت و ترا سلام خواهم کرد سواي جوابِ سلام هیچ بامن نگوئي چون از آنجا بروم نقدِ خود از عطّار بخواه آنچه او بگوید مرا خبر کن * دانشمند موافقِ حکمِ پادشاه بر دوکان عطّار نشست * روزِ چهارم پادشاه با حشمتِ بسیار آن طرف رفت چون دانشمند‌را دید اسپ‌را استاده کرد و بر دانشمند سلام خواند * دانشمند جوابِ سلام گفت * پادشاه فرمود اي برادر گاهي نزدِ من نمي آئي و هیچ احوالِ خود با من نمیگوئي؟ دانشمند اندك سر جُنبانید و دیگر هیچ نگفت * عطّار این همه میدید و مي ترسید * چون پادشاه رفت عطّار دانشمند‌را گفت که هرگاه نقد مرا سپردي کجا بودم و کدام شخص نزدِ من حاضر بود باز بگو شاید فراموش کرده باشم * دانشمند همه احوال باز گفت * عطّار گفت راست مي گوئي حالاً مرا یاد آمد القصّه هزار روپیه دانشمند‌را داد و عُذرِ بسیار نمود *

۹۳ جواني پیرمردي‌را صد دینار سپرد و بسفر رفت * چون باز آمد دینارِ خود خواست * پیرمرد انکار کرد که مرا نداده‌ٔ * جوان همه احوال پیشِ قاضي ظاهر نمود * قاضي پیرمرد‌را طلبید و پرسید که این جوان زر بتو سپرد؟ گفت نه * قاضي جوانرا فرمود کسي گواه داري؟ گفت نه * قاضي پیرمرد‌را گفت سوگند بخور * جوان گریان شد و گفت اورا از سوگند هیچ باك نیست بارها سوگندِ دروغ خورده است * قاضي

جوان را گفت آنوقت که زر باو سپردي کجا نشسته بودي * گفت زیرِ درختي * گفت چرا گفتي که گواه ندارم آن درخت گواهِ تُست نزدِ آن درخت بِرَو و بگو که قاضي ترا مي طلبد * پیر مرد تبسّم کرد * جوان گفت اي قاضي مي ترسم که درخت از حکمِ تو نخواهد آمد * قاضي گفت مُهرِمن ببر و بگو که این مُهرِ قاضي است البتّه خواهد آمد * جوان مُهر قاضي گرفت و رفت * قاضي بعدِ ساعتي از پیر مرد پرسید که آن جوان نزدِ درخت رسیده باشد * گفت نه * چون جوان نزدِ درخت رفت و مُهرِ قاضي نمود و گفت قاضي ترا مي طلبد از درخت هیچ نشنید * غمگین باز آمد و گفت مُهرِ تو درخت‌را نمودم هیچ جواب نداد * قاضي گفت درخت آمد و گواهي داده باز رفت * پیر مرد گفت اي قاضي این چه سخن است هیچ درخت اینجا نه آمد * قاضي گفت راست میگوئي نه آمد لیکن آنوقت که از تو پرسیدم که جوان نزدِ درخت رسید جواب دادي که نرسید * اگر تو زیرِ آن درخت نقد نگرفتي چرا نگفتي که کدام درخت است آنرا نمیدانم * ازین معلوم میشود که جوان راست میگوید * پیر مرد اِلزام یافت و زر بجوان داد *

۹۴ دو برادرِ مفلس بسفر رفتند و در راه کیسهٔ پُر از زر و دو پارهٔ لعل یافتند * برادرِ خورد گفت که غرضِ من حاصل شد حالاً بخانه خواهم رفت * برادرِ بزرگ گفت سَیرِ جهان خواهم کرد * آن زررا قِسمت کردند * برادرِ کلان حِصّهٔ خودرا به برادرِ خورد سپرد و گفت بزنِ من بِدِه * چون او بخانه رسید حصّهٔ برادررا بزنِ او داد مگر لعل نداد * بعدِ سه سال برادرِ کلان از سفر بخانه آمد پارهٔ لعل پیشِ زنِ

F

خود ندید * از برادر پرسید که لعل چه شد * گفت بزنِ تو دادم * گفت او میگوید که نیافتم * گفت دروغ میگوید * آن مرد زنِ خودرا تنبیه آغاز کرد * زن گُریخت و پیشِ قاضي رفت و احوالِ خود باز نمود * قاضي شوهرِ اورا با برادرِ او طلبید و از برادرِ او پرسید که چون لعل باین زن سپردي کسي آن وقت حاضر بود * گفت دو کس * قاضي فرمود بطلب * او آنهارا اندکي نقد داد و گفت با من بیائید و پیشِ قاضي بدروغ گواهي دِهید * القصّه آن هردو گواهي دادند * قاضي شوهرِ آن زن‌را فرمود که بِرَو و از زنِ خود پارهٔ لعل بگیر * زن گریان پیشِ سُلطان رفت و احوالِ خود عرض کرد * سلطان فرمود چرا پیشِ قاضي نمیرَوِي * گفت رفته بودم لیکن بخوبي انصاف نکرد * سلطان آن هردو برادر و گواهانرا طلبید و هریك‌را جُدا کرد و موم داد که بصورتِ آن لعل بسازید * آن هردو برادر یکسان ساختند و آن هردو گواهان بصورتِ مُختلِف * سلطان زن‌را فرمود که تو هم بساز * عرض کرد که لعل گاهي ندیدم چگونه سازم * سلطان گواهانرا سیاست فرمود که اگر راست بگوئید خواهم گذاشت و گرنه خواهم کُشت * ناچار عرض کردند بدروغ گواهي دادیم * سلطان برادرِ خوردرا چند تازیانه زد اقرار کرد که تقصیر کردم * پادشاه بر قاضي عِتاب فرمود که چرا بخوبي انصاف نکردي و لعل‌را بآن زن دِهانید *

۹۵ شخصي کر گلهٔ گوسپند داشت چند گوسپند از آن گله گُم شد براي تلاشِ آنها بصحرا رفت * شخصي را دید که زیرِ درخت خوابیده است اورا بیدار نموده پرسید که گوسپندانِ من درین صحرا گم شده

اند اگر آنها را جائي دیده باشي نشانم دِه * آن مرد هم کر بود دانست که راهِ گم کرده است گفت راهِ راست همین است * او دانست که سراغِ گوسپندان بهمین سمت یافته است پس بگفتهٔ او روان شد و در دلِ خود قرار کرد که اگر گوسپندهارا بیابم گوسپندِ لنگ نذرِ آن مرد خواهم کرد * الحاصل گوسپندانِ گم‌شده‌را یافت و از همان راه برگشت و گوسپندِ لنگ را بر نذرِ آن مرد آورد * او گفت اي بندهٔ خدا هرگز گوسپندِ ترا لنگ نکرده ام تو مرا ناحقّ بدنام مکن * درین گفت وگو بودند که ناگاه سواري در رسید * هر دو کس دویده لجامِ اسپِ او در دست گرفته صورتِ حالِ خود بیان کردند * او هم کر بود دانست که دعویٔ اسپِ من میکنند جواب داد اي یاران شما دعویٔ دروغ میکنید این اسپ‌بچهٔ مادیانِ منست * چندین شاهد دارم عنانِ اسپ را وا گذارید که راهِ خود گیرم * و آن هر دو کس عنانِ اسپِ او گرفته حقیقهٔ خودرا بیان میکردند * او فریاد میکرد که اي ظالمان از خدا به ترسید این کُرّهٔ مادرِ منست * آخرالامر هر سه کر یکجا شده نزدِ قاضي روان شدند * پیش ازین معامله زنِ قاضي از شوهرِ خود جنگ نموده بخانهٔ پدرِ خود رفته بود * هرگاه این هر سه شخص نزدِ قاضي رسیدند قاضي که او نیز کر بود پرسید که چه میگوئید هر سه کس شروعِ بیانِ حالِ خود نمودند قاضي دانست که یك وکیل ودو شاهد از طرفِ زن براي صُلح آمده اند * قاضي جواب داد شما از طرفِ او وکیل وشاهد شده آمده اید اگر او الحال از سر تا پا طلا وجواهر پوشیده بیاید من اورا سه طلاق داده ام هرگز قبول نخواهم کرد

۹۶ شخصي دو هزار روپیه درکیسهٔ سربمُهر به قاضي سپرد و خود بسفر رفت * چون باز آمد کیسهٔ خود همچنان سر بمهر از قاضي گرفت و کشاد فلوس دید * با قاضي مواخذه نمود قاضي گفت بِرَو دروغ میگوئي مرا روپیه‌ها نموده نسپرده بودي کیسهٔ سر بمهر چنان که سپردي باز گرفتي * مردمانِ قاضي اورا راندند * آن شخص پیشِ پادشاه رفت و احوالِ خود عرض کرد * سلطان اندك تامل نموده فرمود که حالاً بِرو و کیسه‌را نزدِ من بدار انصافِ تو خواهم داد * روزِ دیگر پادشاه مسندِ نَوَکه بر تخت بود اندك پاره نمود و بشکار رفت * فرّاشي که آن روز نوبتِ خدمتِ او بود چون مسندرا پاره دید ترسید و لرزه بر اندامِ او افتاد و فرّاشِ دیگررا نمود و گفت اگر پادشاه خواهد دید مرا خواهد کُشت * پرسید که دیگري این سخن شنیده است یا مسندرا دیده؟ گفت نه * گفت خاطر جمع دار درین شهر رفوگري است کامل مسند پیشِ او ببر او اچنان رفو خواهد کرد که کسي نخواهد دریافت * فرّاش بدوکانِ او رفت و مسند برفوگر داد و گفت هرچه بخواهي ترا بدهم لیکن بخوبي رفو کُن رفوگر نیمِ دینار خواست * فرّاش یك دینار اورا بخشید * رفوگر دریکشب مسندرا رفوکرده داد * فرّاش روزِ دیگر آنرا بر تخت گسترد * پادشاه چون مسند درست دید از فرّاش پرسید که این مسند که رفو کرد؟ فرّاش تجاهُل نمود * پادشاه فرمود که هیچ مترس براي مصلحتي این را پاره کرده بودم فرّاش نِشان داد * پادشاه آن رفوگررا طلبید و پرسید که مثل اِین کیسهٔ رفو کردهٔ؟ گفت بلي * گفت اگر آن کیسه‌را بیني شناسي؟ گفت آري * پادشاه کیسه‌را نمود *

رفوگر کیسه‌را شناخت و گفت قاضيء این شهر مرا براي رفو داده بود * پادشاه قاضي‌را طلبید و گفت بر دیانتِ تو اعتمادِ تمام داشتم * بنابر این منصبِ قضا بتو دادم * نمیدانستم که دُزدِي * مالِ این شخص چرا دُزدیدي * گفت ایخداوند که میگوید ؟ گفت من میگویم * پس کیسه‌را نمود و رفورا نشان داد * قاضي شرمنده شد * پادشاه قاضي‌را در زندان فِرستاد و مالِكِ کیسه‌را فرمود که نقدِ خود از قاضي بگیر * قاضي ناچار نقدِ اورا داد *

۹۷ بخیلي خریطهء صد دینار گم کرد * چندانکه طلب نمود کم یافت * گفت هرکه یافته باشد بیارد که ازان ده دینار ازانِ اوست * اتفاقاً بدستِ صالحي افتاد و بخیل را بداد و ایفاي وعده خواست * لئیم که حبهء سیم را بصد جان عزیز میداشت گفت که درین خریطه یك‌صد و ده دینار بود حقِّ خود گرفتهء دیگر چه میخواهي * مردِ نیکوسرشت پیشِ قاضي رفت * قاضي مدعا علَیهِ را طلبید و پرسید که وفاي وعده چرا نمیکني و حقِّ این بیچاره نمیدهي ؟ گفت حقِّ خود گرفته است دیگر چه میخواهد * قاضي خریطه‌اش طلبید دید که همچنان سر بمُهر است * گفت که تو میگوئي در خریطهء مفقود یکصد و ده دینار بود و درین خریطه یکصد دینار است این خریطهء تو نیست از جاي دیگر طلب کن و این کیسه حوالهء این مرد نما که ازانِ دیگر است و مالِكِ این دیگر بوده باشد * و آن مرد را گفت که تو این کیسه را امانت نزدِ خود دار تا که مالِكِ آن پیدا شود *

۹۸ راویانِ اصفار و ناقلانِ اسمار بر جریدهء روزگار چنین ثبت

کرده‌اند که شخصي زري نزدِ صرّافي امانت گذاشت و کلیدِ صندوقچه باخود داشت * پس از مدّتي قطعهء زمیني خرید و بَیعانه داده پیشِ صرّاف آمد و إمانتِ خود طلب کرد * صرّاف مردِ بي‌دیانت خیانت نموده بود پاك منکر گشت * بیچاره حیران بماند و مُرافعه نزدِ وزیر برد * گویند وزیر عاقل و عادل بود کمال دلجوئي اوکرد و صرّاف را طلب داشت و گفت که این کس امانتي بتو سپرده‌است واپس چرا نمي دهي ؟ آن بدنهاد باز هم انکار نمود وزیر گفت کسانِ خود را بِفرِست و صندوقچهء امانت از خانه بطلب * آن مردِ خائِن مُتاملٰ شد و در فرستادنِ کس پس و پیش کرد * وزیر دانست که باعثِ تردّد چیست و سبب تفکّر چه * خود کسي را فرستاد و گفت که از طرف صرّاف کسانِ اورا بگوکه صندوقچهء مقفّل در فلان جا است زودتر بفرستند و اگر اندکي توقّف خواهد شد در زندان خواهم رفت و هرگز نجات نخواهم یافت * مرد از زبانِ صراف هر چه از وزیر شنیده بود اظهار نمود * اهلِ خانه‌اش فوراً صندوقچهء زر حوالهء اوکردند * وزیر زر باو بخشید و صرّاف رِا زجر و توبیخ کرد و از مجلس براند *

۹۹ آورده اند که در زمانِ پیشین خطیبي بزرگ بتفرّجِ بلدان بیرون رفت * هر شام در شهري و هر بامداد بر رهگذري میگذرانید * شبي درسرايء رسید و بساطِ راحت چید بعدِ فراغِ طعام بالاي بام برآمد و هرسو نظري افگند * از دور آوازي موهوم بگوشش رسید * یکي را بدریافتِ آن رَوَان کرد * خادم دیده و شنیده عرض نمود * خطیب نمودِ او بسمع قبول نفرمود خود براثرش روان شد * چون

بدانجا رسید دید که مجرّدي مجذوب است و از عقل بِالکُل مسلوب * بعدِ اداي تعظیم گفت که در چه‌کار مشغولي که از نعم دنیا ملولي ؟ گفت با حریفِ خود بازي میکنم * خطیب گفت حریفِ تو کیست و بازيء تو چیست ؟ گفت حریفِ من خداوندِ گنج است و بازيء من شطرنج * خطیب گفت چرا بازي میکني و خود را در تنگِ پیلِ حرمان مي افگني ؟ مجذوب گفت تا از دست‌بردِ زمان رهائي یابم و کِشْتش نخورم * خطیب گفت از حریفِ خود بازي مییابي یا رخ مي تابي ؟ مجذوب پیاده‌وار سراسیمه و کم ممِ بر زبان آورده گفت گاهي شه مات میکنم و گاهي مات میشوم * خطیب گفت مات بچه طور میشوي و وقتي که مات میکني چه‌کار میکني * مجذوب گفت هنگامي که مات میشوم نقدش بمسکینان نفقه میدهم و گاهي که بازي میگیرم خداوندِ عزّوجلّ از بندگانِ خویش مرا میدهاند اکنون بازيَم از دست رفت و پنجاه دینار خسارت پذیرفت * این بگفت و خریطهء از جیب برآورد وپنجاه دینار ازان بخطیب داد و سر در راهِ خود نهاد * خطیب ازین ماجراي عجیب سخت درماند و ندانست که این زر را چه توان کرد * کام ناکام روان شد و نقد را بفُقَرا داد وازین سانحهء غریب همسایگان را مُطّلع کرد * چون شب درآمد باز همان حالتِ دوشینه معاینه دید و آرزومندِ دیدارِ او گردید * هرگاه نزدِ او رسید بادب سلام نمود * مجذوب جوابِ سلام گفته پردهء راز بکشود و گفت از نفع و زیان چاره نیست * این بار من شاه را مات نمودم و نقدي گران یافتم * خطیب گفت چه قدر یافتي ؟ گفت پانصد دینار بدستِ من

آمد * للحال حاملِ کیسهء نقد توئي که خداي تعالي براي دادنِ آن نزدِ من ترا فرستاده است * و آن روز خطیب نقدِ گران یافته‌بود * بر غیب دانيء او حیران بماند و جبراً و قهراً پانصد دینار حوالهء او نمود * و یقین دانست که این مردِ حیله‌ساز شطرنج‌باز رهزن است * ترسان و لرزان سراسیمه بگریخت و بر ناداني و حماقتِ خود آگاه گردید و کسي را ازین واردات اِطّلاع نکرد که حمل بر حُمق خواهند نمود *

۱۰۰ گویند که در زمانِ نَوشیروانِ عادِل هیچ عِلمي از عِلمِ حِکمت عزیزتر و شریفتر نبود * عُلماء العصر همه مُتّقي و پرهیزگار بودند و خواجه بُزُرجِمِهر حکیم و اُستادِ آن گروه بود * روزي بادشاه خواجه‌را طلب کرد و گفت اي حکیم مي خواهم که سُخني چند مفید در لفظ اندك و در معني بسیار جمع کني که مرا و جمیعِ مردُمان‌را که طالبِ حکمت باشند نفع دِهد و بعدِ من یادگار بماند * بُزُرجِمِهر مهلتِ یك سال طلبید و در مُدّتِ چند انواعِ کلمات‌را جمع کرد و ظفرنامه نام نهاد و بخِدمتِ بادشاه بُرد * بادشاه‌را بغایت خوش آمد و بفرمود تا این سخنان‌را بآبِ زر نوِشتند و در خزانه نهادند ودائم بدان عمل میکرد *

شنیدم که در وقتِ نزعِ روان بهرمُز چنین گفت نوشیروان
که خاطر نگهدارِ درویش باش نه در بندِ آسایشِ خویش باش
نیَاساید اندر دیارِ تو کس چو آسایشِ خویش جوئي و بس
فراخي دران مرزوکشور مخواه که دِلتنگ بیني رعِیّت زشاه
بِرو پاسِ درویشِ مُحتاج دار که شاه از رعِیّت بُود تاجدار
رعِیّت چو بیخست وسلطان درخت درخت اي پسر باشد از بیخ سخت

VOCABULARY.

PERSIAN AND ENGLISH.

اب

آب *āb*, water, splendour.

ابراهيم ادهم *Ibrahīm Adham*, name of a sovereign of Balkh.

آبروي *ābrūe*, honour, reputation.

ابله *ablah*, foolish, *s.* a fool.

آتش *ātish* or *ātash*, fire.

اتفاقا *ittifākan*, accidentally, by chance.

آثار *āsār*, traces, marks : plur. of اثر.

اثبات *isbāt*, confirmation, proof.

اثر *asar*, mark, sign, vestige, effect.

اثنا *asnā*, middle ; *dar asnā-e ān*, or *dar īn asnā* ; in the mean while.

احتراز *ihtirāz*, taking care of one's self.

احمق *ahmak*, foolish, a fool.

احوال *ahwāl*, circumstances, affairs, condition.

احول *ahwal*, a squinting person, one that sees double.

اختيار *ikhtiyār*, choice, power.

آخر *ākhir*, the end, at last ; *ākhir ul amr*, in short, finally.

ادا *adā*, payment, fulfilment ; *adā kardan* or *sākhtan*, to pay, fulfil.

ادب *adab*, politeness, courtesy.

آدم *Adam*, the first man ; hence آدمي, a man, one of the human race.

اسو

ارادت *irādat*, will, inclination.

ارزان *arzān*, cheap, worthy.

آرزو *ārzū*, desire ; *ārzū-mand*, desirous, longing for.

اركان *arkān*, pillars ; *arkān-i daulat*, pillars of state, nobles.

آري *ārī*, yea, yes, yea verily.

از *az*, from, by, with, than.

آزاد *āzād*, free, emancipated.

آزار *āzār*, affliction, vexation.

ازان *azān*, thence, therefore.

آزمودن *āzmūdan*, to try, test.

اسامي *asāmī*, names, or a list of names.

آسايش *āsāyish*, ease, indulgence.

اسباب *asbāb*, means, materials.

اسپ *asp*, a horse ; also اسب.

استاد *ustād*, master, preceptor.

استادن *istādan*, to stand, persist.

استخوان *ustukhān*, a bone.

استماع *istimā'*, hearing.

اسكندر *Iskandar*, Alexander the Great.

اسفار *asfār*, travels : plur. of سفر.

اسم *ism*, a name, noun in Grammar.

اسمار *asmār*, stories, conversations.

آسمان *āsmān*, the sky, the heavens.

آسودن *āsūdan*, to repose, be at ease.

آسيب *āsīb*, trouble, annoyance.

اسير *asīr*, a prisoner, captive.

اصطبل *istabal*, a stable.

اصلا *aslan*, at all, in the least.

اطلاع *itlā'*, information, notice; *ittilā'*, investigating.

اظهار *izhār*, manifestation, pointing out.

اعتماد *i'timād*, confidence, reliance.

اعراب *A'rāb*, an Arab of the desert, or an uncivilized wandering Arab.

آغاز *āghāz*, a beginning.

افتادن *uftādan*, to fall, to happen.

افترا *iftira*, calumny, slander.

آفريدن *āfridān*, to create (root آفرين).

آفرين *āfrīn*, creating, applause, bravo!

افگندن *afgandan*, to cast, throw.

افلاس *iflās*, poverty, destitution.

افلاطون *Aflātūn*, Plato, the Grecian sage.

اقارب *akārib*, relatives, relations.

اقرار *ikrār*, confirmation, confession.

اكثر *aksar*, most, frequently.

اكنون *aknūn*, now, at present.

اگر *agar*, if; اگرچه *agarchi*, though.

ال *al*, the Arabic article "the," prefixed to Arabic nouns.

البته *albatta*, in truth, assuredly.

التفات *iltifāt*, notice, attention.

الحاد *ilhād*, idolatry, infidelity.

الحال *al-hāl*, at present.

الحاصل *al-hāsil*, in short, finally.

الزام *ilzām*, conviction.

القصه *al-kissa*, in short, finally.

الله *Allāh*, God.

الهي *ilahī*, Divine.

اما *ammā*, but, nevertheless.

امان *amān*, protection, safety.

امانت *amānat*, a deposit, a thing entrusted.

امتحان *imtihān*, trial, examination.

آمدن *āmadan*, to come, to be (r. آي).

امر *amr*, matter, affair.

امروز *imroz*, to-day (for *īn-roz*, this day).

آموختن *āmokhtan*, to learn, to teach.

اميد *ummed*, hope.

اميدوار *ummedwār*, hopeful.

امير *amīr*, literally, a commander: a nobleman.

آن *ān*, that, it.

انبار *ambār*, a store, quantity.

انبان *ambān*, a leathern bag.

آنجا *ānjā*, there, in that place.

آنچنان *ānchunān*, such as that, so, even so.

آنچه *ānchi*, that which, whatsoever.

انداختن *andākhtan*, to throw.

اندام *andām*, body, person.

اندر *andar*, within, inside; also اندرون *andarūn*, within.

اندك *andak*, a little; اندكي *andakī*, a small portion.

انسان *insān*, man, the human race.

انصاف *insāf*, justice, one's right.

انعام *in'ām*, a gratuity or present.

انكار *inkār*, denial, refusal.

انگشت *angusht*, the finger.

انگشتري *angushtarī*, a ring.

انگور *angūr*, a grape, raisin.

آنه *āna*, a nominal coin, the sixteenth part of a rupee.

او *ō*, 3d pers. pron. he, she, or it.

آواز *āwāz*, sound, noise, voice.

آوردن *āwardan*, to bring (r. آر or آور).

اول *awwal,* the first.

اولاد *aulād,* family, offspring.

آويختن *āwekhtan,* to cling to, lay hold of.

اهل *ahl,* people.

آهنگ *āhang,* design, intention.

آهنگر *Āhan-gar,* a worker in iron, a blacksmith.

اي *ai,* O!

آيا *āyā,* sign of interrogation.

اياز *Aiyāz,* a man's name.

ايشان *eshān,* plur. of او, they.

ايفا *īfā,* payment, fulfilment.

ايمان *īmān,* faith, conscience.

اين *īn,* pron. he, she, it, or this.

اينجا *injā,* here, in this place.

اينچنين *īnchunīn,* such as this, in this manner.

اينقدر *īnkadar,* to this extent, so much.

اينكه *īnki,* he, &c.; who.

آئنه *ā-īna,* a mirror, times; *har ā-īna,* always, at all events.

ب

ب *ba* (in Arabic, *bi*), a preposition, by, with, in, to; *bi* in fut.

با *bā,* in company with, possessed of.

باد *bād,* the wind; *bar bād dādan,* to give to the wind, to cast away.

بادشاه *bādshāh,* a king.

بار *bār,* a burden; time, as in the phrase *yak bār,* once.

باره *bāra,* behalf; *dar bāra e kase,* in behalf of any one.

باز *bāz,* a hawk: as an adverb, this word signifies iteration or repetition; as, *bāz raftan,* to go back; *bāz kardan,* to put back, or open (a door, &c.); *bāz namūdan,* to declare, shew forth.

بازار *bāzār,* a market.

بازي *bāzī,* a game, play; *bāzī yāftan,* to win the game.

بازيدن *bāzīdan,* to play, gamble.

باعث *bā'is,* cause, reason.

باغ *bāgh,* a garden.

باغبان *bāghbān,* a gardener.

باقي *bākī,* remainder.

باك *bāk,* fear, hesitation.

بالا *bālā,* above, on the top.

بالكل *bilkull,* entirely, in all.

بام *bām,* roof of a house.

بامداد *bāmdād,* in the morning.

بانگ *bāng,* a voice, sound, cry; *bāng zadan,* to call out.

باور *bāvar,* true, creditable; *bāvar kardan* or *dāshtan,* to believe.

باورچيخانه *bāwarchī-khāna,* cook-house, kitchen.

باهم *bāham,* together.

بايستن *bāyistan,* to be proper, necessary: generally used impersonally; as, بايد, it is necessary, &c.

بچه *bacha,* the young of any animal.

بخشيدن *bakhshīdan,* to bestow, forgive, spare.

بخيل *bakhīl,* a miser.

بد *bad,* evil, bad: much used in composition; as, بدخوي *bad-khūe,* of ill-temper; بد روي *bud-rūe,* ill favoured:

بدنام *badnām,* a bad name, reproach.

بدنهاد *badnihād*, depraved, perfidious.

بدانجا *badānjā*, به آنجا, in that place.

بدر *ba-dar*, out, to the door.

بدين *badīn*, for به اين, in this; hereby.

بر *bar*, on *or* upon, for.

برابر *barābar*, literally, breast to breast; equal.

برادر *barādar* and *birādar*, brother.

برادرانه *birādarāna*, worthy of a brother.

بر آمدن *bar-āmadan*, to come up, come to pass.

بر آوردن *bar-āwardan*, to bring up, prolong.

براي *barāe*, for the sake of; *barāe khudā*, for God's sake.

برخاستن *bar-khāstan*, to rise up, to depart.

بردار *bardār kashīdan* or *kardan*, to hang, to crucify.

برداشتن *bar-dāshtan*, to hold up, to carry off.

بردن *burdan* (root, *bar*), to bear, carry away, bring.

بر كندن *bar kandan*, to pluck out, to eradicate.

بركه *birka*, a pond, pool.

برگشتن *bar-gashtan*, to return.

برگماشتن *bar-gumāshtan*, to send forth.

برنج *biranj*, rice.

برو *bar-o*, on him, her, &c.; *biraw*, imperative of *raftan*, go thou.

برهم *barham*, confused, offended, enraged.

برهنه *barahna*, naked, bare.

بريان *biryān* or *buryān*, baked, fried, roasted.

بزرجمهر *Buzurjmihr*, a man's name.

بزرگ *buzurg*, great: applied to age, it means, old, reverential.

بس *bas*, enough; *bas kardan*, to have done.

بساط *bisāt*, a bed, carpet, covering.

بستر *bistar*, a bed, couch.

بستن *bastan* (*band*), to bind.

بسيار *bisyār*, much, many, very.

بعد *ba'd*, at the end, after: generally applied to time.

بقال *bakkāl*, an oil-merchant, a grocer.

بلا *balā*, evil, misfortune, calamity.

بلخ *Balkh*, name of a city.

بلدان *buldān*, cities.

بلع *bala'*, swallowing, devouring.

بلكه *balki*, but, rather, on the contrary.

بلند *buland*, tall, high, great.

بلي *bala*, yea, verily, indeed.

بنابرين *bina-bar-īn*, on this account.

بند *band*, fetter, desire.

بندگي *bandagī*, servitude, submission.

بنده *banda*, a slave, servant.

بوي *bū* or *būe*, fragrance, smell.

بودن *būdān*, to be, exist (r. بو or باش).

به *ba*, by, with, in.

به *bih*, good; frequently used in the sense of بهتر *bihtar*, better.

بهانه *bahāna*, pretence *or* pretext.

بهره *bahra*, a share, portion; utility.

بي *be*, without, deprived of.

بيار *biyār*, imper. *āwardan*, to bring.

بيان *bayān*, explanation, narration.

بيخرجي *be-kharji*, non-expenditure, economy.

بي بي *bībī*, a lady, mistress.

بيعانه *bai'āna*, earnest-money.

بيجا *bejā*, out of place, improper.
بيجگري *be-jigarī*, timidity, cowardice.
بيچاره *be-chāra*, helpless, forlorn.
بيچيزي *be-chīzī*, destitution.
بيحيا *be-hayā*, shameless, impudent.
بيخ *bekh*, root of a tree
بيدار *be-dār*, watchful, awake.
بيرون *berūn*, out, outside.
بيست *bīst*, twenty.
بي عقل *be-'akl*, insane, stupid.
بيكبار *ba-yak-bār*, all at once.
بيگانه *begāna*, a stranger.
بيمار *bīmār*, sick, unhealthy.
بيماري *bīmāri*, sickness.
بيني *bīnī*, the nose.
بيوفا *be-wafā*, faithless, false.
بيهوده *behūda*, foolish, vain.

پ

پا *pā*, the foot.
پاپوش *pā-posh*, foot-covering, slipper.
پادشاه *pādshāh*, a king.
پارچه *pārcha*, a garment.
پارسي *Pārsi* or *Pārasī*, Persian.
پاره *pāra*, a bit, fragment; *pāra kardan*, to break to pieces.
پاس *pās*, a watch of the day or night; *pās-bān*, a sentinel; *pās dāshtan*, to keep watch.
پاسباني *pāsbānī*, keeping watch, protection.
پاك *pāk*, pure, clean; *pāk kardan*, to wipe.
پاكيزه *pākīza*, pure, clean.
پانصد *pānsad*, five hundred.
پختن *pukhtan*, to cook.
پدر *padar* or *pidar*, father.
پر *pur*, full; *par*, a wing or feather.
پرتاب *partāb*, aim; *partāb kardan*, to aim *or* take aim.
پرداختن *pardākhtan*, to finish, to accomplish.
پرده *parda*, a veil, screen.
پرسيدن *pursīdan*, to ask, interrogate.
پرواز *parwāz*, flight.
پروردن *parwardan*, to cherish, to rear.
پرهيزگار *parhezgār*, temperate, pure.
پريدن *parīdan*, to soar, to fly.
پس *pas*, then, after, finally; *pas o pesh kardan*, to demur, make evasion.
پسر *pisar*, a son, a boy.
پسند *pasand*, agreeable; *pasand āmadan*, to be agreeable.
پسنديدن *pasandīdan*, to approve of, to admire.
پشت *pusht*, the back.
پشيمان *pashemān*, penitent, regretful.
پشه *pasha*, a gnat.
پناه *panāh*, aid, shelter, asylum.
پنبه *pumba*, cotton; *pumba-farosh*, cotton-seller.
پنج *panj*, five; *panjum*, fifth.
پنجاه *panjāh*, fifty.
پنداشتن *pindāshtan*, to consider, imagine, believe.
پوست *post*, skin, hide.
پوشيدن *poshīdan*, to put on (a garment), to cover, conceal; *poshanidan*, to cause to be clothed.
پياده *piyāda*, a pedestrian, a pawn (at chess).
پيدا *paida*, manifest, born, created.

پیر *pīr*, old, aged, an old man, an elder.
پیراهن *pīrāhan*, a garment.
پیش *pesh*, before, in front.
پیشینه *peshīna*, former, past.
پیشه *pesha*, a trade, avocation, or profession.
پیک *paik*, a runner or courier.
پیل *pīl*, an elephant; also فیل *fīl*.

ت

تا *tā*, that, so that, until.
تابع *tābi'*, subjected, subdued.
تاجدار *tajdār*, crown-holder, a king.
تار *tār*, dark.
تازیانه *tāziyāna*, a scourge, whip; *tāziyāna zadan*, to flog.
تافتن *tāftan*, to burn, twist, revolve, shine.
تامل *ta-ammul*, meditation, consideration.
تبسم *tabassum*, a smile.
تجارت *tijārat*, traffic, mercantile occupation.
تجسس *tajassus*, search, inquiry.
تجویز *tajwīz*, leave, permission.
تحسین *tahsīn*, praise, commendation.
تحیر *tahayyur*, astonishment.
تخت *takht*, a throne.
تخم *tukhm*, grain, seed-stone.
تدبیر *tadbīr*, arrangement, contrivance.
تراشیدن *tarāshīdan*, to cut off, cut away.
تردد *taraddud*, perplexity, dismay.
ترسانیدن *tarsānīdan*, to terrify: causal of *tarsīdan*, from the root *tars*, fear, dread.
ترسیدن *tarsīdan*, to be afraid.
ترش *tursh*, sad, stern, morose.
ترک *tark*, abandonment, forsaking.
ترک *Turk*, a Turk or Turkomān.
تست *tust*, for *tū-ast*, (it) is of thee or thine.
تشریف *tashrīf*, ennobling; *tashrīf burdan*, to honour an inferior with a visit; to condescend.
تشویش *tashwīsh*, disturbance, trouble.
تصدیق *tasdīk*, verifying, confirmation. of the truth.
تصویر *taswīr*, a picture.
تعاقب *ta'ākub*, pursuit.
تعالی *ta'ālā*, He is exalted, God.
تعب *ta'b*, labour, fatigue.
تعبیر *ta'bīr*, interpretation, explanation.
تعزیت *ta'ziyat*, condolence.
تعظیم *ta'zīm*, magnifying, revering.
تفاوت *tafāwut*, distance, difference (in space).
تفرج *tafarruj*, enjoying or viewing (of scenery, &c.)
تفکر *tafakkur*, thought, contemplation.
تقاضا *takāza*, dunning, demanding.
تقریب *takrīb*, proximity, presence.
تقصیر *taksīr*, delinquency, crime.
تکذیب *takzīb*, accusation of falsehood.
تگ *tag*, bottom, depth; *dar tag*, underneath.
تلاش *talāsh*, search, investigation.
تماشا *tamāsha*, a spectacle, show.
تمام *tamām*, all, entire, the whole.
تنبیه *tambīh*, admonition, reproof.
تنها *tanhā*, alone.
توانستن *tawānistan*, to be able. The root *tawān* is frequently used impersonally, in the sense of 'it is possible,' 'one may.'

تو *tū*, thou.
توبیخ *taubīkh*, blaming, chiding.
توله *tūla*, name of a certain weight.
توقف *tawakkuf*, delay, putting off.
تونگر *tawangar*, powerful, rich.
تهمت *tuhmat*, accusation, calumny.
تهنئت *tahniyat*, congratulation.
تهي *tahī*, empty; *tahī-dast*, empty-handed, destitute.
تیار *taiyar*, ready, prepared.
تیر *tīr*, an arrow.
تیرانداز *tīr-andāz*, an archer; *tīr-andāzī*, archery.
تیز *tez*, sharp, swift, violent.
تیمور *Tīmūr* and *Taimūr*, the far-famed conqueror, commonly called Tamerlane; properly *Taimūr-lang*, *i. e.* Taimur the Lame.

ث

ثبت *sabat*, proof, confirmation.
ثواب *sawāb*, reward, retribution (in a future state).

ج

جا *jā*, place; *ja-kardan*, to occupy a place.
جاسوس *jāsūs*, a scout *or* spy.
جامه *jāma*, a garment.
جان *jān*, soul, life.
جانب *jānib*, side, direction.
جاي *jae*, anywhere, in some place.
جبرا *jabran*, forcibly.
جد *jadd*, grandfather, ancestor.
جدا *juda*, separate, apart.
جرمانه *jurmāna*, a fine *or* penalty.
جریده *jarīda*, a memorandum-book.
جستن *justan* (root جو), to seek.
جگر *jigar*, the liver.
جلاد *jallād*, an executioner.
جلد *jald*, quick, swift.
جماعت *jamā'at*, a number, crowd.
جمع *jam'*, an assembly; *jam' shudan*, to assemble.
جمیع *jamī'*, all, the whole.
جنبانیدن *junibānīdan*, to shake, move (actively); from جنبیدن *junibīdan*, to shake, move (intransitively).
جنك *jang*, war, battle.
جنگل *jangal*, a forest.
جنگلي *janglī*, wild, belonging to the forest.
جواب *jawāb*, answer.
جوان *jawān*, a young man, *juvenis*.
جواهر *jawāhir*, jewels; *jawāhir-khāna*, the jewel-house, treasury.
جوشن *jawshan*, a cuirass, coat of mail.
جوع *jū'*, hunger, appetite.
جهاز *jahāz*, a ship, boat.
جهان *jahān*, the world, an age.
جیب *jaib* or *jeb*, a pocket, purse.

چ

چادر *chādar* or *chādir*, a mantle, sheet, covering.
چاره *chāra*, resource, remedy.
چاشت *chāsht*, the mid-day meal.
چاه *chāh*, a pit, well.
چرا *chirā*, why? wherefore? *chirā-ki*, because.
چراغ *chirāgh*, a lanthorn, lamp.
چریدن *charīdan*, to graze, feed.
چشم *chashm*, the eye.

چقدر *chi-kadar*, to what extent? how much?

چکیدن *chakīdan*, to drop, to fall by drops.

چگونه *chigūna*, what sort? how? why?

چنان *chunān*, like that, such as that.

چند *chand*, some, several.

چندبار *chandbār*, several times, often.

چندین *chandīn*, so much, as much as this.

چنگل *changal*, a hook, a claw.

چنین *chunīn*, such as this, so much.

چون *chūn*, like, when? how? why?

چوب *chob* or *chūb*, a stick, piece of wood.

چه *chi*, that, that which, what? for.

چهار *chahār*, four; *chahārum*, fourth.

چیدن *chīdan* (root چین), to gather, collect.

چیز *chīz*, a thing, an affair.

چیست *chīst*, What is it? for *chi* and *ast* or *hast*.

ح

حاذق *hāzik*, skilful, expert.

حاصل *hāsil*, result; *hāsil kardan*, to acquire; *hāsil shudan*, to be acquired.

حاضر *hāzir*, present, in attendance; *hāzirān*, those attending.

حال *hāl*, condition; *dar hāl*, immediately.

حالا *hālan*, now, presently.

حالت *hālat*, condition, state.

حامل *hāmil*, bearer, carrier.

حبشي *habshī*, an Abyssinian *or* Negro.

حرام زاده *harām-zādah*, unlawful-born, a reprobate.

حرمان *hirmān*, disappointment.

حریف *harīf*, a rival, companion.

حسد *hasad*, envy, malice.

حشمت *hashmat*, pomp, retinue.

حصه *hissa*, a share, portion.

حضرت *hazrat*, presence, Your Majesty, Highness, &c.

حضور *huzūr*, presence, the royal presence, the King's Court.

حق *hakk*, truth, right; *hakk ta'āla*, God Almighty.

حقیقه *hakīka* or *hakīkat*, truth, circumstance.

حکایات *hikāyāt*, stories, tales: plur. of حکایت *hikāyat*, a story, narrative.

حکم *hukm*, order, sentence (of a Judge); rule.

حکمت *hikmat*, sagacity, contrivance.

حکیم *hakīm*, a sage, a doctor.

حماقت *himākat*, folly, stupidity.

حمق *humk*, folly.

حمل *haml*, a burden; *haml kardan*, to impose a burden, to assail.

حوا *Hawā*, Eve, the first woman.

حواله کردن *hawāla kardan*, to give in charge, to consign.

حوض *hawz*, a pond, tank for bathing.

حیا *hayā*, shame, modesty.

حیات *hayāt*, life, lifetime.

حیران *hairān*, astonished, bewildered.

حیرت *hairat*, astonishment.

حیله *hīla*, trick, stratagem.

خ

خادم *khādim*, an attendant, a slave.

خاطر ***khātir***, the heart, soul; ***khātir jam' dāshtan***, to be of good cheer; ***khātir nigāh dāshtan***, to cherish, to win *or* possess the heart.

خاك ***khāk***, the earth, dust.

خالي ***khālī***, bare, empty.

خاموش ***khāmosh***, silent.

خاموشي ***khāmoshī***, silence.

خان ***khān***, an inn; also a Tartar title, lord, ruler; vulgarly, *Cham*.

خانه ***khāna***, a house, mansion.

خانه خرابي ***khāna-kharābī***, ruin of one's house, destruction.

خائن ***khā-in***, a deceiver, treacherous.

خبر ***khabar*** or ***khabr***, news, information.

خبردار ***khabar-dār***, attentive, aware.

خجل ***khajal***, ashamed, abashed.

خجلت ***khajlat***, shame, bashfulness.

خدا ***khudā***, God, a master.

خداوند ***khudāwand***, a lord, master; ***khudawand-i-ganj***, the Lord of the treasure, the Most High.

خدمت ***khidmat***, service, presence.

خر ***khar***, an ass; ***khar-gosh***, a hare.

خراب ***kharāb***, destruction, evil, bad.

خراساني ***khurāsānī***, a native of Khorāsān, the ancient Bactria.

خراندن ***khurāndan***, to cause to eat; to give food, to treat.

خرد ***khurd***, small, little.

خرما ***khurmā***, the fruit of the date-tree.

خروس ***khuros***, a cock.

خريدن ***kharīdan***, to buy, purchase.

خريطه ***kharīta***, a purse.

خزانه ***khizāna***, a treasury.

خسارت ***khasārat***, loss, damage.

خسپيدن ***khuspīdan***, to sleep.

خسرو پرويز ***Khusrū*** or ***Khusrau Parwīz***, a celebrated king of Persia.

خشم ***khishm*** or ***khashm***, anger, indignation.

خشنود ***khushnud***, also خوشنود, content, joyful, pleased.

خصي ***khasī***, a goat.

خط ***khatt***, a letter, an epistle.

خطا ***khatā***, an error, failure, missing.

خطيب ***khatīb***, a preacher.

خلاص ***khalās***, liberation, freedom.

خلاف ***khilāf***, the contrary, opposite.

خلعت ***khil'at***, a dress of honour.

خلوت ***khalwat***, privacy, retirement.

خليدن ***khalīdan***, to pierce into the flesh (as a thorn), to prick.

خفتن ***khuftan***, to sleep (r. خسپ ***khusp***).

خنثي ***khunsa***, a Hermaphrodite.

خنده ***khanda***, smile, laughter.

خنديدن ***khandīdan***, to smile, laugh.

خو or خوي ***khū*** or ***khūe***, temper, disposition.

خواب ***khāb***, sleep, dream. V. Gr. p. 12. *a*.

خوابيدن ***khābīdan***, to sleep.

خواجه ***khāja***, a master, merchant.

خوار ***khār***, devouring: used in composition; as, ***bisyār-khār***, a glutton.

خواستن ***khāstan***, to wish, will, desire, (its aorist, from the root ***khāh***, is used as an auxiliary in the formation of the future tense).

خواندن ***khāndan***, to read, to call.

خواهر ***khāhar***, a sister.

خوب ***khūb***, good, beautiful.

خوبي ***khūbī***, goodness, beauty, virtue.

c

خود *khud*, self, a friend.

خور *khur*, food.

خورد *khurd*, small, little.

خوردن *khurdan*, to eat, to swallow.

خوش *khush*, pleasant, good; *khush āmadan*, to be agreeable, to be welcome.

خوشي *khushī*, joy, pleasure.

خوشدامن *khushdāman*, a mother-in-law, a wife's mother.

خوشنود *khushnūd*, pleased, satisfied.

خوشه *khūsha*, a bunch of grapes.

خويش *khesh*, self. Vid. Gr. p. 12. *b*.

خيانت *khiyānat*, treachery, dishonesty.

خيريت *khairiyat*, welfare, safety.

د

دادن *dādan*, to give, pay (r. ده *dih*).

دار *dār*, the gallows, a gibbet: in composition it means possession.

داروغه *dārogha*, the head man of an office.

داشتن *dāshtan*, to possess, hold, have.

دامن *dāman*, skirt of a garment.

دانا *dānā*, wise, prudent.

دانستن *dānistan*, to know, to think.

دانشمند *dānishmand*, wise, learned.

دانه *dāna*, a grain, seed.

دائم *dā-im*, always, perpetual.

دختر *dukhtar*, a daughter, a damsel.

دخل *dakhl*, entrance.

در *dar*, a door; also, in, into, at; *ba-dar*, out, to the door.

دراز *darāz*, long, distant; also *dirāz*.

درامدن *dar-āmadan*, to enter.

دراويختن *dar-āwekhtan*, to contend, grapple with.

دربان *darbān* (also *darwān*), a door-keeper, a porter.

درخت *darakht*, a tree, a stalk.

درد *dard*, pain (bodily or mental).

درسيدن *dar-rasīdan*, to arrive, enter.

درست *durust*, right, true.

درم *diram*, money, a small silver coin.

در ماندن *dar-māndan*, to be destitute, to be "in a fix," to be weary.

دروازه *darwāza*, a door, a gate.

دروغ *durogh*, a lie, falsehood; *durogh-go*, a liar.

درون *darūn*, in, inside, within.

درويش *darwesh*, poor, a religious mendicant.

درهم *dar-ham*, together, contracted; *rūe dar-ham kashīdan*, to be offended, to frown.

دريا *daryā*, the sea, a river.

دريافت *daryāft*, discovery, comprehension.

دريافتن *dar-yāftan*, to discover, understand.

دريچه *darīcha*, a window.

درين *dar-īn*, in this.

دزد *duzd*, a thief.

دزدي *duzdī*, theft; *ba-duzdī raftan*, to be stolen, to go by theft.

دزديدن *duzdīdan*, to steal.

دست *dast*, the hand.

دستار *dastār*, a turban.

دست برد *dast-burd*, victory (in play, war, &c.)

دستور *dastūr*, rule, custom.

دشمن *dushman*, an enemy.

دشمني *dushmanī*, enmity, hostility.

دشنام *dushnām*, abuse.

دعا *du'ā*, prayer, supplication.

دعوي or دعوا *da'wā*, a claim, request.

دفتر *daftar*, a volume, a book.

دفع *daf'*, repelling, warding off.

دفن *dafn*, burying, hiding under ground.

دل *dil*, the heart, mind; *dil-tang*, distressed in heart; *dil juī*, seeking the heart, kindness, courtesy.

دلق *dalk*, a dress worn by religious mendicants.

دلو *dalw*, a bucket.

دم *dam*, a breath, a moment; *dum*, the tail.

دمّل *dummal*, also دنبل *dumbal*, a tumour, a sore.

دنبال *dumbāl*, stern, rear, behind.

دندان *dandān*, a tooth.

دنيا *dunyā*, the world, the present life.

دو *dū*, two.

دوا *dawā*, medicine, cure.

دو پهر *du-pahr*, the second watch, noon, midnight.

دور *dūr*, distance, far, remote.

دوزخ *dozakh*, hell.

دوست *dōst*, a friend, companion.

دوستي *dōstī*, friendship.

دوش *dōsh*, the shoulder; last night.

دوشينه *doshīna*, of *or* during last night.

دوكان *dūkān*, a shop, office.

دولت *daulat*, wealth, fortune.

دوم *duwum*, the second, secondly.

دويدن *dawīdan*, to run.

دويم *dūyum*, the same as *duwum*.

ده *dah*, ten; *dih*, a village; also, give, root of *dādan*, to give.

دهانيدن *dihānīdan*, to cause to give.

دهقان *dihkān*, a villager, a peasant.

ديار *diyār*, a country, kingdom.

ديانت *diyānat*, probity; *diyānatdār*, honest.

ديدار *dīdār*, a sight, an interview.

ديدن *dīdan* (root بين *bīn*), to see, experience.

ديروز *dīroz*, yesterday.

ديشب *dī-shab*, yesternight.

ديگر *dīgar*, another, again.

دينار *dīnār*, name of a coin, a denarius.

ديوار *dīwār*, the wall of a house, &c.

ديوانه *dīwāna* or *devāna*, mad.

ذ

ذائقه *zā-ika*, the palate, taste.

ذو القرنين *zū-lkarnain*, two-horned, an epithet applied by the Arabs to Alexander the Great.

ر

راحت *rāhat*, tranquility, enjoyment.

راز *rāz*, a secret.

راست *rāst*, straight, right, true.

راندن *rāndan*, to drive away, send, dismiss.

راوي *rāwī*, a narrator, historian.

راه *rāh*, road, path.

رحم *ruhm* or *ruhum*, mercy, pity.

رحمن *rahmān*, merciful, compassionate.

رحيم *rahīm*, gracious, forgiving.

رخ *rukh*, the cheek; the castle at chess.

رخصت *rukhsat*, dismissal, leave.

رزاق *razzāk*, The Bestower, bountiful.

رسانيدن *rasānīdan*, to send, convey.

رسن **rasan,** a rope, string.
رسیدن **rasīdan,** to arrive, reach.
رشید **rashīd,** wise, upright.
رضا **rizā,** satisfaction, consent.
رعایت **ri'āyat,** observance; **ri'āyat kardan,** to observe, maintain.
رعیت **ra'īyat,** subject, people.
رفتن **raftan** (root رو **raw**), to go, move.
رفو **rafū,** repair, mending.
رفوگر **rafūgar,** a repairer, mender.
رنج **ranj,** sorrow, vexation, pain.
رنجیدن **ranjīdan,** to grieve, vex.
رو **rū** or روي **rūe,** the face; **rū-ba-rū,** in presence, face to face.
روان **rawān,** going; the soul, spirit.
روباه **robāh,** a fox; **robāh-bacha,** a fox-cub.
روپه **rūpa,** silver, a rupee.
روپیه **rūpiya,** a rupee, a silver coin, value about two shillings.
روز **roz,** a day, time in general.
روزگار **rozgār,** lifetime, the world, fortune.
ره **rah,** a road, path; **rahguzarī,** a highway; **rahzan,** a highwayman.
رهانیدن **rahānīdan,** to release, rescue: causal of رستن **rastan** (r. ره **rah**).
ریختن **rekhtan,** to spill, destroy.
ریز **rez,** a crumb, particle.
ریسمان **rīsmān,** a rope, chord.
ریش **rīsh,** the beard, a suit of clothes for festive occasions; **resh,** a sore, a wound.

ز

زاده **zāda,** born, a descendant: used in composition; as, **shāh-zāda,** born of a king, a prince.
زاغ **zāgh,** a crow, a raven.
زاهد **zāhid,** a holy man, a hermit.
زبان **zabān,** the tongue, a language.
زبون **zabūn,** a captive; a dupe.
زجر **zijr,** hindering, force, threat.
زدن **zadan** (r. زن **zan**), to strike, inflict.
زر **zar,** gold, money, wealth.
زشت **zisht,** hideous, ugly; **zisht-rūe,** of an ugly face; **zisht-khūe,** of a vile temper.
زمان **zamān,** time, season, an age.
زمین **zamīn,** earth, land, region.
زن **zan,** a wife, woman.
زنا **zina,** fornication.
زندان **zindān,** a prison, a jail.
زندقه **zindaka,** idolatry, impiety.
زندگی **zindagi,** existence, life.
زنده **zinda,** alive.
زنهار **zinhār,** take care! beware!
زوجه **zauja,** a wife.
زود **zūd,** soon, quick, speedily.
زور **zor,** force, violence.
زیاده **ziyāda,** more, increase.
زیان **ziyān,** loss, damage.
زیر **zer,** beneath, below.
زیرا **zīrā** or **zīrā-ki,** because, since.
زیستن **zīstan,** to live, exist.
زین **zīn,** a saddle.

س

ساختن **sākhtan,** to make, frame, form.
ساعت **sā'at,** an hour, an instant.
سال **sāl,** a year.
سان **sān,** mode, manner; **chi-sān,** how?
سانحه **sāniha,** revelation (of the marvellous).
سائس **sā-is,** a groom, a manager.

ساية *sāya*, shade, shelter.

سبب *sabab*, cause, reason.

سبو *sabū*, a cup, jar, pot, pitcher.

سپر *sipar*, a shield, target.

سپردن *supurdan* or *sipurdan* (r. سپار *sipār*), to entrust, consign.

ستودن *sitūdan*, to praise.

ستون *sutūn*, a pillar, prop.

سخاوت *sakhāwat*, liberality, munificence.

سخت *sakht*, hard, strong, violent.

سخن *sukhan* or *sukhun*, a word, a matter, a thing in general.

سر *sar*, the head, top; a design: *sirr*, a secret.

سرا or سراي *sarā* or *sarāe*, an inn.

سراپا *sar-ā-pā*, from head to foot, entirely.

سراسيمه *sarāsīma*, disturbed, delirious.

سراغ *surāgh*, a sign, mark, trace.

سربمهر *sar ba muhr*, sealed up at the top.

سرراه *sar-i-rāh*, a road, path.

سرشت *sirisht*, nature, constitution.

سركار *sarkar*, a headman, Court, Government.

سرود *surod*, a song, melody.

سزا *sazā*, desert, punishment.

سفر *safar*, a journey, voyage.

سكندر *sikandar*, Alexander the Great.

سگ *sag*, a dog.

سلام *salām*, salutation, peace, safety.

سلطان *sultan*, a supreme ruler, emperor, king.

سليس *salīs*, easy, familiar, not abstruse.

سنگ *sang*, a stone, a weight.

سوار *suwār*, a horseman; *suwār shudan*, to be mounted.

سوال *su-āl*, asking, begging, a question.

سواي *siwāe*, except, besides.

سوختن *sokhtan*, to burn, to be inflamed.

سوداگر *saudāgar*, a merchant.

سوگند *saugand*, an oath; *saugand khurdan*, to swear, literally, "to eat an oath." Vide Story 18.

سوم *siwum*, the third, thirdly.

سويت *sawiyat*, equality, fairness.

سه *sih*, three.

سياست *siyāsat*, punishment.

سياه *siyāh*, black.

سيخ *sīkh*, a spit.

سير *sair*, a walk, a journey.

سيله *sīla*, a blow, a buffet.

سيلي *sīlī*, a blow, a slap.

سينه *sīna*, the bosom, breast.

سيوم *siwum*, the third, thirdly.

ش

شادي *shadī*, marriage, rejoicing.

شاعر *shā'ir*, a poet.

شام *shām*, evening.

شاه *shāh*, a king, monarch.

شاهد *shāhid*, a witness, a bystander.

شاهزاده *shāh-zāda*, a king's son, prince.

شايستن *shāyistan*, to be fit, proper.

شب *shab*, night, evening.

شتاب *shitāb*, haste, speed.

شتر *shutur*, a camel.

شجاعت *shajā'at*, valour, prowess.

شخص *shakhs*, a person.

شدن *shudan*, to be, become.

شرح *sharh*, interpretation, commentary.

شرط *shart*, stipulation; wager.

شرم *sharm*, shame.

شرمنده ***sharmanda***, ashamed, confounded, abashed.

شروع ***shurū'***, beginning, attack.

شريف ***sharīf***, noble, eminent, holy.

شريك ***sharīk***, a partner, companion.

شستن ***shustan*** (r. شو ***shū***), to wash, cleanse.

شش ***shash***, six.

شطرنج ***shatranj***, the game of chess.

شعله ***shu'la***, a flame.

شفاعت ***shifā'at***, intercession, deprecation.

شفقت ***shafkat***, pity, compassion, affection.

شك ***shakk***, doubt.

شكار ***shikār***, hunting, prey, game.

شكايت ***shikāyat***, complaint.

شكر ***shukr***, thanks; ***shakar***, sugar.

شكست ***shikast***, defeat, disaster.

شكستن ***shikastan*** (root شكن ***shikan***), to break, defeat.

شكم ***shikam***, the belly.

شگون ***shugūn***, an omen of good.

شما ***shuma***, you: plur. of تو, thou.

شمشير ***shamshīr***, a sword, scimitar.

شناختن ***shinākhtan*** (r. شناس ***shināṣ***), to know, recognise.

شنيدن ***shinīdan***, to hear; also ***shunīdan***, ***shanīdan***.

شور ***shor***, noise, tumult, uproar.

شوهر ***shohar*** and ***shauhar***, a husband.

شهد ***shahd***, honey, sugar.

شهر ***shahr***, a city; a lunar month.

شهمات ***shah-māt***, check-mate; literally, "king dead."

شير ***sher***, a lion, a tiger.

شيرين ***Shīrīn***, name of a lady, wife of Khusrū Parwīz.

شيشه ***shīsha***, a phial, a glass.

شيطان ***Shaitān***, Satan, the Devil.

ص

صاحب ***sāhib***, a companion, a lord, master: in composition, it means endowed with; as, ***sāhib-kamāl***, possessed of perfection. Vid. Gr. p. 28. *b*.

صاف ***sāf***, pure, clear, evident.

صباح ***sabāh***, morning, dawn of day; ***'ala-s-sabāh*** or صباحا ***sabāhan***, early in the morning.

صبح ***subh***, the morning, dawn, Aurora.

صحرا ***sahrā***, a desert, a plain.

صد ***sad***, a hundred.

صراف ***sarrāf***, a banker, money-changer.

صرف ***sarf***, changing, turning; ***sirf***, pure, merely.

صعوه ***sa'wa***, a kind of sparrow.

صف ***saff***, drawing up (men) in ranks; ***saffzada***, mustered, arrayed.

صلاح ***salāh***, advice, counsel.

صلح ***sulh***, peace, concord.

صندوق ***sandūk***, a chest, box, trunk; ***sandūkcha***, a small box.

صورت ***sūrat***, form, figure, face.

صيد ***said***, hunting, prey, game.

ض

ضامن ***zāmin***, a surety, sponsor.

ضعيف ***za'īf***, infirm, weak, poor.

ضيافت ***ziyāfat***, a feast, invitation.

ط

طالب *tālib*, asking, studious.

طبابت *tibābat*, the medical art.

طبيب *tabīb*, a doctor, physician.

طرف *taraf*, extremity, direction, side.

طعام *ta'ām*, food, eating.

طعمه *tu'ma*, food, dinner.

طفل *tifl*, an infant, a child.

طلا *tilā*, gold, gold fringe.

طلب *talab*, petition, demand, wages; *talab dāshtan*, to search.

طلبيدن *talabīdan*, to seek for, call.

طمع *tama'*, avidity, desire.

طور *taur*, mode, manner, condition.

طوطي *tūtī*, a parrot.

طول *taul* or *tūl*, length, height, duration.

طي *tayy*, traversing, travelling; *tayy kardan*, to traverse, pass over.

طيب *tayyib*, good, agreeable.

ظ

ظالم *zālim*, tyrannical, oppressive.

ظاهر *zāhir*, clear, evident, certain.

ظرف *zarf*, a vessel, a vase, bottle.

ظريف *zarīf*, witty, learned, graceful.

ظفرنامه *Zafar-nāma*, Book of Victory, the title of several Persian works.

ع

عادل *'ādil*, upright, just.

عاري *'ārī*, naked, destitute, bare.

عاشق *'āshik*, a lover, loving.

عاقل *'ākil*, wise, intelligent.

عالم *'ālam*, the world, time, state; *'ālim*, learned, wise.

عبادت *'ibādat*, worship, adoration.

عبارت *'ibārat*, style (in writing), sense.

عتاب *'itāb*, reproof, anger.

عجائب *'ajā-ib*, marvels, wonders.

عجب *'ajab*, wonderful, strange.

عجيب *'ajīb*, rare, wonderful.

عدالت *'adālat*, justice, equity; *'Adālat-panāh*, Asylum of Justice.

عدل *'adl*, justice, integrity.

عذر *uzr*, excuse, apology.

عرب *'Arab*, an Arab, applied to those who dwell in towns.

عرض *'arz*, a representation, speech.

عزو جل *'Azza wa jalla*, May He be honoured and glorified! *i.e.* God.

عزيز *'azīz*, dear, precious.

عصا *'asā*, a staff, a bludgeon.

عطار *'attār*, a druggist, a perfumer.

عطر *'itr*, odour, perfume.

عفو *'afū*, forgiveness, indulgence.

عقد *'akd*, an agreement, alliance.

عقل, *'akl*, reason, sense, wisdom.

عقوبت *'akūbat*, punishment, torture.

علامت *'alāmat*, a sign, mark, token.

علم *'ilm*, knowledge, science.

علوم *'ulūm*, sciences (plur. of last word).

علي *'Alī*, a man's name.

علي *'ala*, on *or* at.

عمر *'umr*, lifetime, age.

عمل *'amal*, action, conduct, rule.

عنان *'inān*, a bridle, the reins.

عنايت *'ināyat*, a favour, bounty.

غ

غالب *ghālib*, prevailing, victorious.

غايت *ghāyat*, the extreme, extremely.

غرض *gharaz*, wish, design; *al-gharaz*, in short, finally.

غرفه *ghurfa*, a window, a parlour.

غرور *ghurūr*, pride, haughtiness.

غريب *gharīb*, poor, strange, rare.

غصه *ghussa*, grief, anger.

غضب *ghazab*, anger, vengeance.

غلام *ghulām*, a slave, a boy.

غله *ghalla*, corn, grain.

غليظ *ghalīz*, cross, rude, sordid.

غم *gham*, grief, care, anxiety.

غمگين *ghamgīn*, sorrowful.

غيب *ghaib*, secrecy, invisibility; *ghaib-dānī*, knowledge of what is secret.

ف

فارسي *Fārsi*, also پارسي *Pārsī*, Persian.

فايده *fā-ida*, profit, benefit.

فتح *fath*, an opening, a victory.

فجر *fajr*, the dawn, morning.

فراخور *farākhūr*, suitable to, proportional, in accordance with.

فراخي *farākhī*, extension, abundance.

فراش *farrāsh*, a chamberlain.

فراغ *firāgh*, leisure, cessation.

فراموش *farāmosh*, forgetfulness.

فراوان *farāwān*, great, important.

فربه *farbih*, fat, flourishing.

فردا *fardā*, to-morrow.

فرزند *farzand*, a son, a child.

فرستادن *firistādan*, to send.

فرصت *fursat*, opportunity, leisure.

فرمان *farmān*, a command, edict.

فرمودن *farmūdan*, to order: it is used in the sense of "to speak, say," on the part of a superior; also, to do, make. Vide Gram. p. 64. *o.*

فرو *faro* (before a vowel, فرود *farod*), down, below, underneath.

فروختن *farokhtan* (r. فروش), to sell.

فروش *farosh* (in composition), a seller.

فرياد *faryād*, a complaint, a cry for aid.

فريادي *faryādī*, a complainant, plaintiff.

فريب *firīb* or *fareb*, deception; *fareb dadan*, to impose on.

فريفتن *fireftan*, to deceive, to mistake.

فصل *fasl*, season; a section.

فقرا *fukarā*, poor people: plur. of

فقير *fakīr*, a poor person, a mendicant.

فكر *fikr*, thought, anxiety.

فلاطون *Falātūn*, the same as *Aflātūn*, Plato.

فلان *fulān*, some one, such a one.

فلوس *fulūs*, coins of small value, *cowries, dibs.*

فوج *fauj*, an army.

فورا *fauran*, instantly.

فهميدن *fahmīdan*, to understand.

في *fī*, in: used only in Arabic phrases.

فيل *fīl*, an elephant (also پيل *pīl*).

ق

قابو *kābū*, means, opportunity.

قاضي *kāzī*, a Judge.

قبول *kabūl*, consent, agreement.

قتل *katl*, killing, execution.

قد *kad*, length, stature, figure (also *kadd*).

قدر *kadar*, measure, quantity, extent.

قدرت *kudrat*, power, daring.

قديم *kadīm*, old, ancient.

قرار *karār*, settlement, agreeing.

قرض *karz* or *kirz*, a loan, a debt.

قرضدار *karz-dār,* a debtor.

قسم *kasam,* an oath ; *kasam-khurdan,* to swear ; literally, "to eat an oath," hence the pun in Story 18.

قسمت *kismat,* division, partition.

قصد *kasd,* purpose, design.

قصدا *kasdan,* purposely, intentionally.

قصر *kasr,* a citadel, palace.

قضا *kazā,* fate, destiny, death.

قطعه *kit'a,* a section, part, stanza.

قلاده *kilāda,* a collar, ornament for the neck.

قمار *kimār,* dice *or* any game of hazard.

قوت or قوة *kūwat,* strength, firmness.

قوي *kawīy,* strong, powerful.

قهرا *kahran,* by force, on compulsion.

قيد *kaid,* thraldom, imprisonment.

قيمت *kīmat,* price, value.

ك

كار *kār,* business, use, affair.

كاغذ *kāghaz* or *kāghiz,* paper, a letter.

كامل *kāmil,* perfect, entire, accomplished.

كام *kām,* desire, intention ; *kām nā-kām,* willingly *or* unwillingly.

كاه *kāh,* straw, hay, grass.

كباب *kabāb,* meat, fried or roasted.

كتاب *kitāb,* a book, an epistle.

كثيف *kasīf,* course, thick.

كجا *kujā,* where? what place? how?

كج مج *kaj-maj,* crooked, cross purposes.

كدام *kudām,* what one? which?

كر *kar,* deaf.

كرايه *kirāya,* hire, fare, rent.

كردن *kardan* (r. كن *kun*), to do, to make.

كس *kas,* a person, any, some one.

كسب *kasb,* gain, art, trade.

كشادن *kushādan,* to open, disclose.

كشاكش *kashākash,* contention, battle.

كشت *kisht,* check, a term at chess.

كشتزار *kishtzār,* a corn-field.

كشتن *kushtan,* to slay, kill, extinguish.

كشودن *kushūdan,* to open.

كشيدن *kashīdan,* to pull, draw, delineate.

كفر *kufr,* impiety, infidelity.

كفن *kafan,* a winding-sheet, a shroud

كلان *kalān,* great, aged, elder.

كلمات *kalimāt,* words, sayings.

كلوخ *kulūkh,* a clod, brick.

كلي *kullī,* all, the whole.

كليد *kalīd,* a key.

كم *kam,* little, few, scarce.

كمال *kamāl,* perfection, accomplishment.

كمان *kamān,* a bow.

كنار *kinār,* side, bosom, margin.

كناره *kināra* or *kanāra,* side, brink, shore of the sea or river.

كندن *kandan,* to dig, extract, tear up.

كنيز *kanīz,* a maiden, a maid-servant.

كوتاه *kotāh,* short, small.

كوتوال *kotwāl,* a magistrate, judge.

كور *kōr* or *kūr,* blind.

كوز *kūz,* a hump, hump-backed.

كه *ki,* who? that, used as a conjunctive particle, like the Greek ὅτι, after verbs signifying to think, speak, tell, &c.

كهن *kuhan,* also كهنه *kuhna,* old, worn.

كيست *kīst,* for كه, and هست or است, who is?

كيسه *kīsa* or *kesa,* a purse, a bag.

d

گ

گاه *gāh,* time, also place (in composition).

گدا *gadā,* poor, a beggar, mendicant.

گذاشتن *guzāshtan,* to quit, forsake, leave.

گذر *guzar,* a pass, passing.

گذشتن *guzashtan* (r. گذر *guzar*), to pass, pass by.

گر *gar,* if: contraction of اگر.

گران *girān,* heavy, important, valuable.

گربه *gurba,* a cat.

گرد *gird,* around; *gard,* dust.

گردانيدن *gardanīdan,* to circulate, to effect, cause to become.

گردن *gardan,* the neck.

گرديدن *gardīdan,* to turn round, to be, become; also گشتن (r. گرد *gard*).

گرسنه *gursina,* hungry, famished.

گرسنگي *gursinagī,* hunger, starvation.

گرفتار *giriftār,* caught, involved, a capture.

گرفتن *giriftan,* to catch, seize, to begin: so in German, *fangen,* to catch; *anfangen,* to begin.

گرم *garm,* warm, hot, passionate.

گرما *garmā,* heat, hot season.

گرو *giraw,* a pawn, pledge, wager.

گروه *guroh,* a troop, band, company.

گريختن *gurekhtan, girekhtan,* to flee, run away.

گريستن *girīstan,* to weep, bewail; so *giriyān shudan,* to be weeping.

گستردن *gustardan,* to spread, arrange.

گفتن *guftan* (r. گو *gū*), to say, speak.

گفت وگو *guft-ō-gū* or *guftgū,* conversation, chit-chat.

گله *gala* or *galla,* a flock, herd.

گم *gum,* lost, missing.

گماشتن *gumāshtan,* to consign, send forth.

گناه *gunāh,* fault, crime, sin.

گنج *ganj,* a treasure.

گندم *gandum,* wheat.

گواه *gawāh,* a witness, an evidence.

گواهي *gawāhī,* testimony, evidence.

گورستان *goristān,* a burying-ground.

گوسپند, also گوسفند, *gospand, gosfand,* a sheep, a ram, a goat.

گوش *gosh,* the ear.

گوشت *gosht,* flesh, meat.

گونه *gūna,* mode, manner, form.

ل

لا *lā* (a negative particle, Arab), no, not: used as a prefix; as in لاجواب *lā-jawāb,* without an answer, silenced.

لائق *lā-ik,* worthy, proper, fit for.

لباده *labāda* or *lubāda,* a thick outer garment, a boat-cloak.

لت *lat,* a thump, a blow.

لجام *lijām* or *lajām,* a bridle, the reins.

لذيذ *lazīz,* sweet, pleasant.

لرزه *larza,* a shaking, trembling, tremor.

لطيف *latīf,* good, pleasant, kind.

لطيفه *latīfa,* a witty saying, pleasantry.

لعل *la'l,* a ruby, a gem.

لفظ *lafz,* a word, a vocable.

لقمه *lukma,* a morsel, a mouthful.

لك *lak,* a numeral expressive of 100,000.

لگام *ligām* or *lagām,* a bridle.

لنگ *lang,* lame, an epithet applied to the celebrated Tīmūr.

ليكن *lekin,* but, yet, nevertheless.

م

ما *mā*, we: plur. of the 1st person.

مات شدن *māt-shudan*, to be checkmated; *māt kardan*, to give checkmate.

ماجرا *mā-jarā*, an accident, event, what has passed or occurred.

مادر *mādar*, a mother.

ماده *māda*, a female.

ماديان *mādiyān*, a mare.

مال *māl*, wealth, treasure, property.

مالك *mālik*, a master, possessor.

ماليدن *mālīdan*, to rub, to anoint.

ماندن *māndan*, to remain, continue.

ماه *māh*, the moon, a month.

ماهي *māhī*, a fish.

ماهي گير *māhī-gīr*, a fisherman, a fish-catcher.

مبادا *ma-bādā*, May it not be! God forbid!

مبالغه *mubālagha*, a strenuous effort, urgency, hyperbole.

مبلغ *mablagh*, a sum (of money), price.

متامل *muta-ammil*, thoughtful, contemplative.

متدين *mutadayyin*, orthodox, religious.

متعجب *muta'ajjib*, astonished, wondering.

متفكر *mutafakkir*, meditating, thoughtful.

متقي *muttakī*, sober, pious, temperate.

مثل *misl*, similitude, like, likeness.

مجذوب *majzūb*, abstracted, absent.

مجرد *mujarrad*, solitary, alone.

مجلس *majlis*, an assembly, company.

محبوبه *mahbūba*, loved, esteemed.

محتاج *muhtāj*, in want of, destitute.

محروم *mahrūm*, excluded, disappointed.

محظوظ *mahzūz*, pleased, delighted.

محقر *muhakkar*, vile, trifling, contemptible, worthless.

محكم *muhkam*, strong, firm, firmly.

محمد *Muhammad*, a man's name, the celebrated prophet of the Muslims.

محمود *Mahmūd*, a man's name, a king of Ghiznī, about A.D. 1000.

محو كردن *mahw-kardan*, to wipe out, efface.

مختار *mukhtār*, absolute, a free agent.

مختلف *mukhtalif*, diverse, various.

مدت *muddat*, a space of time.

مدح *madh*, praise, eulogy, encomium.

مدرسه *madrasa*, a college, school.

مدعي *mudda'ī*, plaintiff, accuser.

مذكور *mazkūr*, mentioned, aforesaid.

مرا *marā*, me, to me: Dative or Accusative of من, I.

مرافعه *murāfa'a*, citing before a Judge, a law-suit.

مرتبه *martaba*, step, dignity, a time.

مرثيه *marsiya*, an elegy, a funeral oration.

مرد *mard*, a man, a hero.

مردم *mardum*, a person, man.

مردن *murdan* (root مير *mīr*), to die.

مرده *murda*, plur. *murdagān*, dead.

مرز و كشور *marz o kishwar*, empire, kingdom.

مرغ *murgh*, a fowl, a bird.

مسافر *musāfir*, a traveller, a stranger.

مساكن *masākin*, habitations, places of abode.

مست *mast*, intoxicated, wanton, furious.

مستي *mastī*, intoxication.

مسجد *masjid*, a mosque, or any place of worship.

مسخره ***maskhara***, a jester, a buffoon.

مسکین ***maskīn***, humble, poor, wretched.

مسلوب ***maslūb***, seized, stripped, erred.

مسند ***masnad***, a throne, a prop.

مشت ***musht***, the fist, a blow.

مشغول ***mashghūl***, occupied, engaged in.

مشهور ***mash-hūr***, celebrated, notorious, public.

مصاحب ***musāhib***, a companion, a friend, courtier.

مصلحت ***maslahat***, good counsel, good policy, the best course to adopt *or* the best thing to be done.

مصور ***musawwir***, a painter.

مطبخ ***matbakh***, the kitchen, a place for cooking.

مطرب ***mutrib***, a musician, a minstrel.

مطلع ***muttali'***, inspecting, seeing.

مع ***ma'***, with, in the company of.

معاف ***mu'āf***, forgiven, spared, free.

معامله ***mu'āmala***, business, transaction, affair.

معاینه ***mu'āyana***, beholding, seeing clearly.

معذور ***ma'zūr***, excused, excusable.

معروف ***ma'rūf***, celebrated, well known.

معلم ***mu'allim***, a doctor, teacher, sage.

معلوم ***ma'lūm***, known, evident.

معني ***ma'nā*** or ***ma'nī***, sense, meaning, fact, a sacred record.

مغل ***Moghal*** or ***Mughal***, name of a Tartar or Scythian tribe.

مفلس ***muflis***, poor, indigent.

مفلسي ***muflisī***, poverty, destitution.

مفيد ***mufīd***, useful, salutary.

مقام ***makām***, place, residence.

مقدار ***mikdār***, quantity, space, measure.

مقراض ***mikrāz***, shears, scissors.

مقفل ***mukfal***, locked, bolted, stingy.

مگر ***magar***, but, unless, only.

مگس ***magas***, a fly.

ملاقات ***mulākāt***, meeting, interview.

ملعون ***mal'ūn***, accursed, the Evil One.

ملول ***malūl***, fatigued, vexed.

ملك ***milk***, property; ***mulk***, a country, kingdom; ***malik***, a king; ***malak***, an angel.

ممکن ***mumkin***, possible, practicable.

من ***man***, the 1st pers. pronoun, I.

منادي ***manādi***, a proclamation.

منازعت ***munāza'at***, contention, litigation.

مناقشه ***munākasha***, quarrel, dispute.

منتخب ***muntakhab***, a selection.

منجم ***munajjim***, an astrologer.

منزل ***manzil***, an abode, a stage, an inn.

منصب ***mansab***, a high station, dignity.

منع ***man'***, prohibition, prevention.

منقار ***minkār***, a beak, bill.

منکر ***munkir***, one who denies, refuses.

مواخذه ***mu-ākhaza***, taking satisfaction, calling to account.

موافق ***muwāfik***, conformable to, like.

موت ***maut***, death.

موجب ***mūjib***, cause, motive, reason.

موجود ***maujūd***, existing, found, ready.

موصوف ***mausūf***, praised, qualified, described.

مولوي ***mawlawī***, a doctor of the Muhammadan law.

موم ***mūm*** or ***mom***, wax, a wax candle.

موهوم ***mawhūm***, imaginary, fancied.

موي ***mūe***, hair, wool, fur.

مهر *muhr*, a seal, a seal ring; *mihr* friendship, love.
مهربان *mihr-bān*, kind, beneficent.
مهلت *mihlat*, delay, space of time.
مهمان *mihmān*, a guest, a stranger.
مي *maī*, wine, spirituous liquor.
ميان *miyān*, middle, interval, space.
ميخ *mekh*, a peg, a tent pin *or* pole.

ن

نا *nā*, a negative particle to adjectives, participles, and infinitives.
نابينا *nābīnā*, not seeing, blind.
ناچار *nāchār*, helpless, without remedy.
ناحق *nāhakk*, unjust, untrue.
ناخوش *nākhush*, displeased.
ناقل *nākil*, a narrator, historian.
ناگاه *nā-gāh*, suddenly, unexpectedly.
نالش *nālish*, lamentation, complaint.
نالشي *nālishī*, a complainant, plaintiff.
نام *nām*, name, renown.
نامردي *nā-mardī*, unmanliness, cowardice.
نان *nān*, bread, a loaf.
نايب *nā-ib*, a lieutenant, deputy.
نجات *najāt*, freedom, salvation, escape.
نديم *nadīm*, a companion, a courtier.
نذر *nazr*, a present *or* offering.
نر *nar*, a male.
نزد *nazd*, near, about, in the possession of.
نزديك *nazdīk*, near, close to.
نزع *naz'*, removal; *naz'i rawān*, the last breath, the soul's departure.
نسبت *nisbat*, affinity, connection.
نشان *nishān*, a trace, mark.
نشانيدن *nishānīdan*, to place, cause to sit down; also نشاندن.
نشستن *nishastan* (r. نشين *nishīn*), to sit, stop, settle.
نصف *nisf*, the half, middle.
نصيحت *nasīhat*, advice, admonition, a sermon.
نظر *nazar*, the sight, the eye.
نعم *nu'm*, prosperity, good fortune.
نعمت *ni'mat*, a blessing, favour, prosperity.
نفع *naf'*, gain, profit, advantage.
نفقه *nafaka*, maintenance, salary.
نقاش *nakkāsh*, a painter.
نقد *nakd*, ready money, cash.
نقش *naksh*, a painting, a picture.
نقصان *nuksān*, damage, deficiency, loss.
نكته *nukta*, a point, a quaint saying.
نگاه *nigāh*, a look, observation; *nigāh dāshtan*, to watch over, preserve; *nigāh-dār*, a preserver: also used as an interjection, beware! have a care!
نماز *namāz*, prayer, worship.
نمود *namūd*, an appearance, index.
نمودن *namūdan*, to appear, to shew, to make.
نوبت *naubat*, time, turn, opportunity.
نوشتن *navishtan* (r. نويس *navīs*), to write; also نبشتن *nabishtan*.
نوشيروان *Naushīrwān*, name of a Persian king, famed for equity.
نوكر *naukar*, a servant, slave.
نويسنده *navīsanda*, a writer.
نه, the negative particle, not; *nuh*, nine.
نهادن *nihādan*, to place, put, apply.
نيابت *niyābat*, the office of a deputy, deputyship.

نيز **nīz**, also, even, likewise.
نيست **nīst**, he, she, it, is not.
نيك **nek**, good, beautiful, right.
نيكنامي **nek-nāmī**, fame, renown.
نيكو **neko**, good, excellent.
نيم **nayam**, I am not.
نيم **nīm**, the half, the middle.

و

و **wa** (sometimes *o*), and, but.
وا **wā**, back, reverse.
واپس **wāpas**, back, returned.
واردات **wāridāt**, events, occurrences.
وجب **wajab**, a span, about nine inches.
وجه **wajh**, face, mode, manner.
وزارت **wazārat**, the office of a *wazīr* or minister.
وزير **wazīr**, a minister, the king's vicegerent.
وصف **wasf**, description, quality.
وطن **watn** or **watan**, one's native country, home.
وعده **wa'da**, a promise, a vow, pledge.
وعظ **wa'z**, a sermon, admonition, lecture.
وفا **wafā**, fidelity, sincerity.
وفات **wafāt**, death, decease.
وقت **wakt**, time, hour, season.
وكيل **wakīl**, an agent, deputy, factor.
وي **wai**, 3d pers. pron. he, she, it.

ه

هارون **Hārūn**, a man's name.
هارون الرشيد **Hārūn-ar-rashīd**, "Hārūn the Wise," one of the *Khalīfas* of Baghdād.
هجو **hajw**, ridicule, satire, lampoon.
هر **har**, every, each.
هرچند **harchand**, although, notwithstanding.
هرچه **harchi**, whatsoever.
هركه **harki**, every one who, whosoever.
هرگاه **hargāh**, every time, whenever.
هرگز **hargiz**, ever, at all, on any account.
هرمز **Hurmuz**, name of a Persian king.
هزار **hazār**, a thousand.
هزيمت **hazīmat**, flight, defeat.
هستن **hastan**, to be, to exist; a defective verb. Vide Gram. p. 48. *c*.
هشت **hasht**, eight.
هم **ham**, even, also, (in composition) together.
همان **hamān**, that very, even that; *hamān-dam*, that very instant.
همچو **hamchū**, even as, like.
همچنان **hamchunān**, such as that, even so.
همراه **ham-rāh**, a companion, along with.
همسايه **ham-sāya**, a neighbour.
همه **hama**, all, every one.
هميشه **hamesha**, always.
همين **ham-īn**, even this, this very.
هندو **Hindū**, an Indian, a Hindū.
هندوستان **Hindūstān**, India.
هنوز **hanoz**, yet, still, at present.
هنگام **hangām**, time, season.
هوا **hawā**, the air, the sky.
هيچ **hech**, any, at all, in the least.

ي

يا **yā**, either, or.
ياد **yād**, memory, remembrance.
يادگار **yādgār**, a memorial.
يار **yār**, a friend.

یافتن *yāftan*, to find, obtain.
یعنی *ya'nī*, that is to say, namely.
یقین *yakīn*, certainty, for certain.
یك *yak*, one, a *or* an: sometimes joined to the following word; as,
یکجا *yak-jā*, in one place, together.
یکدرم *yak-diram*, a *diram*, a small coin.
یکدیگر *yak-dīgar*, one another.
یکسال *yak-sāl*, one year, a twelve-month.
یکسان *yaksān*, equal, similar, identical.
یکهزار *yak-hazār*, a thousand.
یکیک *yak-yak*, or یکبیك *yak-ba-yak*, one by one, individually, one after another.

NOTICE TO THE LEARNER.

It has been our anxious endeavour that the preceding Vocabulary should contain all the words occurring in the forty pages of the Extracts. Before the Student commences reading and translating the latter, it is of course understood that he has made himself thoroughly acquainted with the inflections of the Noun and Verb. He ought also to commit to memory the Pronouns and simple Prepositions, as these are necessarily of frequent occurrence in a language. He should endeavour to remember the rules and *exceptions* respecting the formation of the verbal roots from the Infinitives, which will, by consequence, enable him to find the latter in the Vocabulary, where all Verbs are to be sought for under the Infinitive. When the Infinitive has any anomaly in the formation of the root, the latter is always added in the Vocabulary; as, دیدن *dīdan* (r. بین *bīn*), "to see."

In order to compress the Vocabulary into as small a compass as possible all *superfluities* have been eschewed. The short vowel-marks, &c. have been omitted, which has enabled us to give more words in each page; and the pronunciation of each word is given in the Roman character. The mere indication of the various parts of speech has been deemed superfluous:

for instance, we should consider it an insult to the Reader's understanding to say that پدر *padar*, "a father," is a *substantive masculine*. Lastly, we have avoided all distinction between Persian and Arabic words, as a matter of no earthly consequence to the Student at this early stage of his progress: nor have we been at all ambitious of attaining that very cheap reputation for profound learning, arising from exhibiting the Arabic roots along with their cognates in Hebrew, Syriac, and Ethiopic, each in its proper character, with a view to astonish the eyes of the vulgar.

In order that the Student may not waste time in useless search, he must be careful to reduce each word to its simple form, before he looks for it in the Vocabulary, by stripping it of such prefixes and additions as it may happen to have. The prefixes are, 1st, بَ, used as a preposition before a noun, and, in verbs, prefixed, as بِ or بيِ, to the Future, and, redundantly, to the Preterite. 2dly, نَ or نيَ, and مَ or ميَ, prefixed to verbs to denote negation (Gram. p. 48. No. 40). 3dly, مي or همي prefixed to verbs, to denote the Present and Imperfect Tenses.

The ordinary affixes are, 1st, the ي, denoting unity, &c. (Gram. p. 30. No. 29); as, شخصي "a certain person" (in the Vocabulary, look for شخص). 2dly, The plural terminations, ان, گان, يان, and ها (Gram. p. 25. No. 25.), together with the termination را. 3dly, The terminations added to form the various persons of the verb; and, lastly, pronominal affixes, مَ, تَ, شَ. Vide Grammar, p. 33. No. 32, and more fully in the Syntax. By attending to these few hints the learner will be spared some trouble, and the Vocabulary will incur less censure on the score of deficiency.